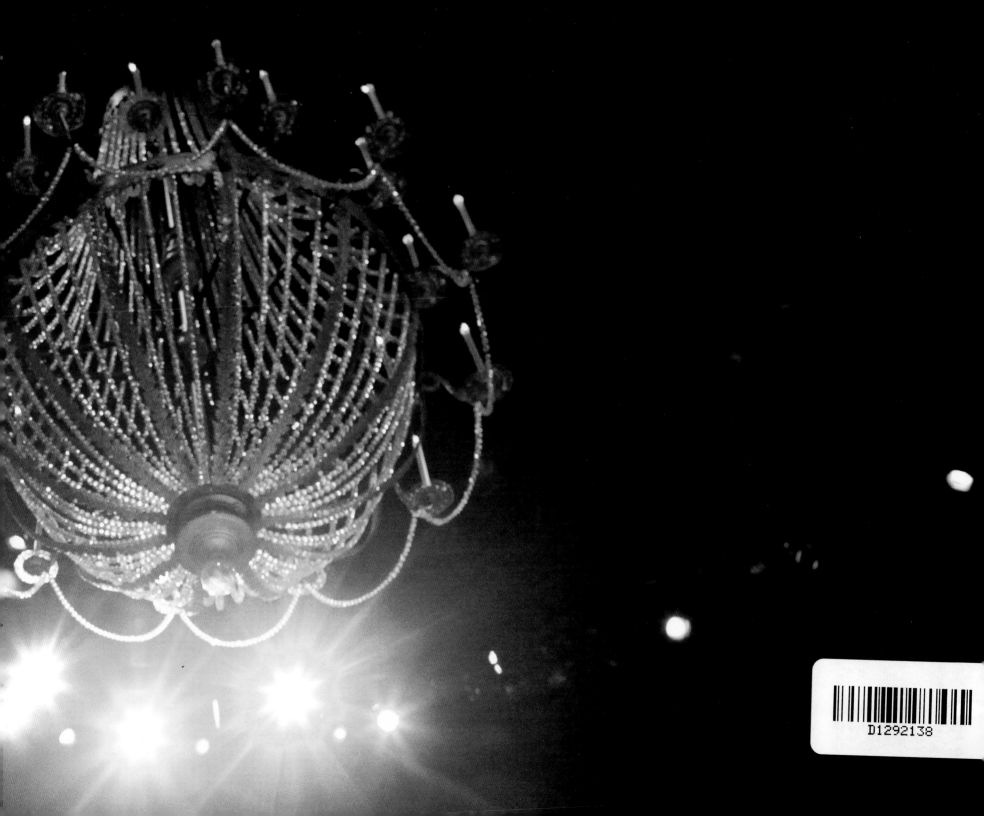

Stratford
Behind the Scenes

By Don Gillmor
Foreword by Lloyd Robertson
Photography by Erin Samuell

Stratford Behind the Scenes

Creative direction, and graphic design and print production management, by Andy Foster
Designed and typeset, with additional photography and retouching, by Krista Dodson

Additional text by Robert Blacker, Andrea Jackson, Francesca Marini and David Prosser
Additional photography by Richard Bain, Burdett Photography, Jane Edmonds, Kerry Hayes, David Hou, Terry Manzo and Scott Wishart

Cover: Sara Topham (Célimène) backstage during a performance of *The Misanthrope* (2011).
Back cover: Company members Victor Dolhai and Jaz Sealey prepare to make an entrance in *The Misanthrope* (2011).

Library and Archives Canada Cataloguing in Publication

Gillmor, Don
Stratford behind the scenes / by Don Gillmor ; foreword by Lloyd Robertson ; photography by Erin Samuell.

ISBN 978-0-9730509-2-9

1. Stratford Shakespeare Festival. 2. Theater—Production and direction—Ontario—Stratford.
3. Theatrical companies—Ontario—Stratford. I. Samuell, Erin II. Stratford Shakespeare Festival III. Title.

PN2306.S7G56 2012   792.09713'23   C2012-902383-3

Printed and bound in Canada by TC Transcontinental Printing

Stratford Shakespeare Festival
55 Queen Street
Stratford ON
N5A 6V2
stratfordshakespearefestival.com

Table of Contents

"What's past is prologue"

– *The Tempest*, Act II, scene 1

Foreword:
The City of Stratford

By Lloyd Robertson

Gathering on and around the well-travelled path of Stratford's storied Avon River is a tradition for city residents and visitors alike. The cameras click the familiar pictures: family picnics on lush green lawns with children playing among the weeping willows, older brothers and sisters paddling canoes, parents and grandparents sharing stories and admiring the majestic elegance of the swans; these are the idyllic summer scenes captured through the generations.

Today, looking up from the Avon and above a sweeping expanse of lawn, as if to guard this tranquil portrait of life, is the centre of an artistic enterprise that transformed a fading southwestern Ontario city right before our eyes. Sixty years ago, a new Stratford began to soar to its rightful place in the constellation of major world cultural destinations; its destiny fulfilled more than a century after its founding.

For those of us lucky enough to launch our lives in the "classic city," the pleasant ambience and easy rhythms of daily life made it the perfect place to grow up. In Stratford, with a population under twenty thousand in the forties and early fifties, the river and beautifully sculpted Shakespearean gardens, as well as a downtown that encouraged neighbourliness, were always nearby. My friends and I went to schools named Shakespeare, Romeo, Juliet or Falstaff. Around every corner we were reminded of the bard who always seemed to be sitting on our shoulders. But it would take some time before his full-blown spirit would make a measurable impact on the city and its inhabitants, even though he had elbowed his way into the consciousness of the tiny settlement on the Little Thames River very early in its life.

Lloyd Robertson at the Festival Theatre.

In 1832, a picture of Shakespeare was handed to William Sargint, proprietor of the former Shakespeare Hotel on Ontario Street, and from there the story grew. We can imagine Thomas Mercer Jones, who was a director of the Canada Company, a British land development firm set up to colonize the area, saying to Sargint: "Display this prominently; he will be our inspiration." Jones wanted his legacy to incorporate the names and historical markers of his beloved homeland, and Stratford-upon-Avon, England, was obviously one of them.

Sixty years ago, a new Stratford began to soar to its rightful place in the constellation of major world cultural destinations

The Little Thames was soon renamed the Avon; the settlement became Stratford and all was in readiness for the greening of what the Nations in Bloom Festival has called "the prettiest city in the world."

In the early years, the locals would know their town was named after the birthplace of a famous English playwright, but the knowledge likely brought little more than mild interest or detached amusement. More important was the realization that Stratford was taking advantage of the burgeoning age of steam that ruled the rails from 1870 to 1960. It stood at the crossroads of main railway trunk lines—no better place for the repair and maintenance of those huge and complex steam engines. They could be pulled into the Stratford locomotive repair shops and pushed back into active service quickly. Thousands of skilled workers and labourers converged on the city. Over the years, "the Shops" employed more than forty percent of Stratford's workforce. My father came in from a nearby family farm for steady work on the big machines.

The city's blue-collar traditions grew as furniture factories sprouted in the east end, and for decades, in spite of industrial strife that saw the army come in to quell rioting in the "Dirty Thirties," Stratford thrived as an industrial centre.

If today's residents listen for the sound of the trumpets to herald the opening of each Festival Theatre play, we were treated to the shop whistles calling workers to their jobs and signalling the beginning and end of the work day at eight in the morning and five in the afternoon.

But inevitable change was to burst the bubble. Steam faced extinction from diesel power, the "Shops" were heading for closure, and the furniture factories, facing stiffer competition, were laying off workers and scaling back. By the 1950s, Stratford was spiralling into dark economic times.

However, unlike many other cities in North America, it would never become a victim of industrial-age decay and sink into despair. Dedicated residents had kept the city's classic heritage alive through the years, pushing to keep the hometown beautiful as a tribute to the bard for whom it was named.

William Shakespeare was never forgotten. There were the many concrete reminders of his plays and characters all over the city, as well as parks, gardens and walkways.

At just the right moment, as if by magic, Shakespeare was to play his central role. The bard had long inspired the mild-mannered but determined Tom Patterson, a Stratford native and business journalist who had grown up with a dream of seeing his hero's plays performed in the Canadian Stratford on the banks of the Avon. He had often walked the river's path to soak up its calming presence while his mind buzzed with plans to persuade the city his idea had merit. There were lots of skeptics asking: "How could a bunch of actors and their pals save Stratford?"

Patterson persisted, and with the help of sympathetic officials and residents, he managed to link up with Tyrone Guthrie, the most influential British theatre director of the times. Guthrie was impressed with Patterson's passion and big idea; Guthrie could make it work.

In what seemed like the blink of an eye, a huge canvas tent was rising on the banks of the Avon, and on July 13, 1953, Guthrie's friend, internationally acclaimed actor Alec Guinness, strode onto a three-sided thrust stage in front of a hushed audience of over two thousand seated round about. He opened with fifteen words from Shakespeare's *Richard III*—"Now is the winter of our discontent / Made glorious summer by this sun of York"—that would echo through international theatre chronicles as the first chapter of a brave new venture.

For those sitting in the temporary tent in the early times, train whistles competed with the actors for the audience's attention. It was the railway's dying gasps near the end of an era. Alec Guinness and fellow actors, riding their bicycles through city streets, were soon mixing with the dwindling numbers of denim-clad workers as the motif of the city began to change.

Did Shakespeare save Stratford? The numbers tell the story: five hundred thousand people visit every year; the Festival employs a thousand people and generates $139 million in annual economic activity.

Even more than that, the Festival's success inspired the creation of a twenty-first-century city that takes advantage of its location and international renown to attract new industry for a new age.

And after sixty years, the Festival follows its established patterns of the seasons. In the following pages, Don Gillmor takes us inside those patterns and their purposes as the crowds come and go, from the blooms of spring to the flaming colours of autumn. They applaud the players, marvel at Stratford's beauty and gather on the banks of the Avon as the old river gently flows and documents another year in the city's history.

The Festival Theatre at sunrise.

The Festival's success inspired the creation of a twenty-first-century city, attracting new industry for a new age

A Fleeting Glimpse of Greatness

In his foreword to this book, renowned broadcaster Lloyd Robertson sets the scene for us by describing the Stratford of the early 1950s, when the Festival had its birth. In the pages that follow, author Don Gillmor leaps over the intervening six decades to take us firmly into the present.

As we debated how best to celebrate in print our milestone sixtieth season in 2012, we decided that, rather than retelling the remarkable but already well-known story of the Festival's origins and subsequent growth into North America's leading classical repertory theatre, we might offer you something else: a glimpse behind the scenes of the Festival as it is today, so that you might gain some insight into how playbills are put together and how productions reach the stage.

What follows is necessarily *only* a glimpse, and by no means a comprehensive one. Besides the people whose names and images appear in this book, there are literally hundreds of others—not only artists, artisans and technicians, but also administrators, marketers, fundraisers and all the others who contribute in their own indispensible ways to the Festival's success—whose talents deserve to be celebrated, whose stories and insights call out to be shared. A dozen more books like the one you hold in your hand could easily have been compiled, had we had world enough and time.

In the opening lines of *Henry V*, the Chorus asks the audience to use their imaginations to transcend the inherent limitations of the theatre: to accept that one soldier on stage may represent a thousand. Likewise, it is impossible to encompass in a single volume Stratford's extraordinary wealth of talent, skill and dedication; we ask, therefore, that you "piece out our imperfections with your thoughts" and allow the words and images of a few to serve as emblems of the many. We hope you will enjoy this peek behind the scenes, and that it will leave you eager to discover much, much more about the extraordinary undertaking that is the Stratford Shakespeare Festival today.

Antoni Cimolino
General Director

Des McAnuff
Artistic Director

Photographer Andrew Eccles shoots General Director Antoni Cimolino (left) and Artistic Director Des McAnuff for the Festival's 2012 Visitors' Guide.

Chapter One

One Brief Shining Moment: The Season Ends

In late October 2011, the season is almost over, the twelve productions winnowed to six. The leaves have turned; Stratford is at its most picturesque. Some of the more than one thousand people employed by the Stratford Shakespeare Festival have decamped, off to other theatres, other countries. The directors and designers are gone; the army of actors, wigmakers, shoemakers, technicians, fight captains, carpenters, seamstresses, dressers and crew has thinned.

At 9 a.m. the stagehands descend on the stage at the Festival Theatre. They are more benign-looking than their rock-and-roll roadie counterparts—fewer Led Zeppelin T-shirts and tattoos—but their role is similar. A dozen men in white hardhats start disassembling the dramatic set of *Twelfth Night*, which played the night before. Designed by Debra Hanson, the set looks heavy and permanent, but its massive wooden arch—representing the frame of a shattered mirror—is revealed to be sections of Styrofoam that were specially cut by a hot-wire saw: an electrified wire stretched between two computer-controlled plotter heads that can precisely cut intricate patterns. The large leaves and flowers were hand-cut and glued on. It was then covered in cheesecloth and painted to look like wood.

The lights are lowered, the arch taken apart, the massive twenty-foot sculptural framing pieces tipped onto their sides and wheeled away on dollies. Five men work on the dark floor, which is coated in a basketball-

Scenic carpenter Hal Harley sweeps the *Camelot* floor.

Top: Crew member Walter Sugden (left) and Technical Director Andrew Mestern check one of the motorized platforms used in *Twelfth Night*. Above left: Crew member Michael Walsh checks out sound equipment. Above right: Stage crew set up for *Camelot*. Facing page: Crew members Rory Feore (on ladder) and Brad Stephenson assemble the tree for *Camelot*.

court clear finish, using long wrenches to loosen the rotor locks that join all the sections. The pieces are loaded onto dollies and then the plywood subfloor is taken up. After an hour, there is no trace of *Twelfth Night*.

For a minute or so, the famous thrust stage that was pioneered by founding director Tyrone Guthrie and founding designer Tanya Moiseiwitsch stands unadorned—or at least a version of it. It has been altered several times over the decades. When Guthrie came to Stratford in 1952, he brought this idea with him. Then, as now, most of the world's stages were proscenium arches. The thrust stage put the actors into the audience; it broke down the formal barrier of the proscenium. "The plays," Guthrie wrote in his memoir, *A Life in the Theatre*, "therefore seem more intimate and the verse does not make the huge demand upon technical virtuosity as when it has to carry to the back of an opera house." The shape was designed so that the spectators are part of the performance: they see not just the actors but one another.

"The master stroke of Tanya's design," says Stratford's present Artistic Director, Des McAnuff, "is not the structures on the stage, which have changed since the beginning, but the relationship it gives actor to audience. Listen to the intimacy that Christopher Plummer brings to his performances here, and you will understand the genius behind Tanya's design."

As the changeover continues, a new subfloor is locked into place, a seventeen-foot revolve (a circular section of the stage that can rotate like a giant turntable) is set up, and the medieval-patterned floor of *Camelot* is laid on top. The curtains are set in place, balconies hoisted and fastened, the baroque trees raised on cables. The sets are stored in three semi-trailers that are pulled up to the side of the building, a necessity given the limited space backstage and the absence of wings in a thrust-stage configuration.

Two hours after the stagehands arrived, the romantic confusion of *Twelfth Night* has given way to the romantic idealism of *Camelot*. First produced in 1960 with Richard Burton as Arthur and Julie Andrews as

Top: Backstage at a performance of *Camelot*, Geraint Wyn Davies (King Arthur) hugs (from left) wardrobe attendant Brigitte Nazar, Kaylee Harwood (Guenevere) and stage manager Cynthia Toushan. Above left: Lucy Peacock (Morgan le Fay). Above right: Sandy Winsby, doubling for Merlyn in *Camelot*'s opening montage, with Clara the hawk.

Guenevere, Lerner and Loewe's last Broadway show together actually made its debut in Canada: its first preview was at Toronto's O'Keefe Centre (now the Sony Centre for the Performing Arts). The original cast album topped the charts for sixty blissful weeks, before rock and roll swept it away.

Across town, at the Avon Theatre, *Jesus Christ Superstar* is playing. The two musicals act as bookends for the 1960s, which started with the crisp buttoned-down world of John F. Kennedy and ended with the pulsing rock of *Superstar*, which first appeared as a concept album in 1970. Between them, Vietnam, the Summer of Love and a disillusioned generation.

An hour after the *Camelot* set is in place, yellow buses filled with schoolchildren begin to arrive: fourteen-year-olds who have been briefed on the nobility of King Arthur's Round Table and the glaring absence of that quality in modern politics. The kids sprawl on the grounds outside the theatre, debating the greatness of Lady Gaga, eating their sandwiches, staging mock ninja battles on the manicured lawn, lost in their iPods.

At 12:30 p.m., an hour and half before the matinée performance, assistant stage manager Zeph Williams patrols backstage, making sure all the props are in place and working. He checks that the torch actually lights; ticks off his list of flowers, helmets, weapons and thrones; makes sure there are wet wipes to clean up after the hawk. He examines the muriatic acid and ammonia that sit, ominously, in separate containers, waiting to be mixed together in Act II to produce fog.

At 1:25 the last of the actors arrive and sign in. They go to their dressing rooms, where their stage clothes have been sprayed with vodka to keep them fresh, a trick learned from a Russian ballet company. Vodka kills the bacteria that cause unfortunate odours without introducing any odour of its own.

Geraint Wyn Davies (King Arthur) comes early before each performance to do vocal exercises with a coach. He rarely does musicals ("once every eight years or so"), and although the singing parts for Arthur are slightly

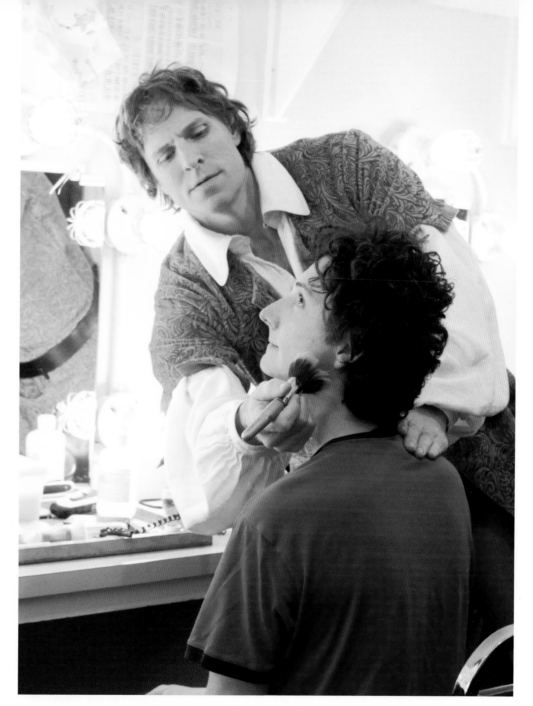

Dan Chameroy (Sir Dinadan) pretends to help Mike Nadajewski (Mordred) with his makeup.

talky and suited to his rich baritone, he likes to open his breathing, establish the highs and lows before each show. He isn't fazed by the schoolchildren, who he says are much better behaved than they once were. In the past, when scenes changed during the blackouts, all kinds of things were hurled by children in the anonymous darkness.

In one of the rehearsal halls, the fight captain supervises the warm-up for the fight scenes in the show. They run through these scenes twice before every performance, once at half speed and once at show speed. The actors use surprisingly heavy aluminum swords that don't have a cutting edge but are nevertheless dangerous. "A bit more energy," the fight captain says, eating a sandwich. "Good, good."

At three minutes before curtain, a member of the ensemble collapses and can't go on. The stage manager, Cindy Toushan, bustles down the corridor, announcing, "Dominique's out, Laurin's in." Laurin Padolina is the female swing, someone who can play any part in the women's ensemble. There is a male swing and a female swing in every musical. There are understudies for the principal parts, but the swing must be able to do any of the ensemble parts, known as "tracks." In musicals that are very physical and more prone to mishap (*West Side Story*, for example), there can be as many as four swings. This is the ninety-sixth performance of *Camelot*, and the production has seen its share of illness, emergencies and injury, none of it visible to the audience.

By 1:40 the audience start to take their seats, a crowd that includes 350 schoolchildren. More than sixty thousand students come to Stratford each year from as far away as Boca Raton, Florida, Oklahoma City and Wheeling, West Virginia. They come from Toronto, Ottawa and Sherbrooke, Quebec. They are surprisingly enthusiastic but don't always get the textual jokes, especially in Shakespeare. They tend to howl at the sight gags, though, and sometimes laugh at odd moments (when someone dies, for example).

The house lights dim, the spot comes up and Merlyn

Facing page: During the interval of *Camelot*, the stage crew prepare to hoist Guenevere's tent. The fabric is packed inside the crown of the tent. Above, top: Jonathan Winsby (Lancelot) and Matt Alfano (Kabuki Knight) do a fight warm-up prior to the performance. Above left: Company member Julius Sermonia. Right: Geraint Wyn Davies (King Arthur).

Left: Jonathan Winsby (Lancelot) is suited up by wardrobe attendant William C. Kraft. Right: Knights of the Round Table enter from the stage left vomitorium.
Facing page: Brent Carver dons a beard for his role as Merlyn.

enters, wearing a heavy leather falconry glove. In the corridor behind the upper balcony, Clara is waiting for her cue. Clara is a Harris's Hawk (*parabuteo unicintus*), a popular falconry bird because of its temperament and effectiveness, and she sits irritably on the arm of Julia, the hawk wrangler from Hawkeye Bird and Animal Control. Clara is playing a transmogrified King Arthur, part of Merlyn's strategy of turning the future king into various animals to give him a richer perspective on life.

A light in the hallway is the cue. When it goes off, Zeph Williams opens the door and Julia untethers Clara, who leaps through the opening like a missile, swoops low over the audience with her considerable wingspan and lands on Merlyn's forearm to grab the raw quail meat that awaits. It took a month to train Clara for the role; at first, she just flew threateningly around the auditorium. Clara has an understudy named Barb, and when the two of them aren't engaged in the theatre, they have the unglamorous job of keeping seagulls away from nearby landfill sites.

Backstage, ensemble members are stretching and practising pirouettes. Brent Carver, who plays both Merlyn and Pellinore, is being fitted into a harness in which he will rise through a very narrow opening in the ceiling, hauled up by an electric winch. The other dangling scenery (two trees and two large cones) and the revolving stage are controlled by crew member Tim Hartman, who sits in a small room backstage at a computer.

On stage, Arthur and Guenevere (Kaylee Harwood) meet at a sculptural tree, banter romantically and sing about Camelot and the joys of maidenhood. They flirt and become confused: the tremors of love.

Meanwhile, Merlyn is drawn into the cave of a beautiful water nymph, where eternal sleep awaits. This is Carver's cue to ascend, and he is winched up on the cables without a hitch, escorted by a complex play of light. Up in the cupcake, as it's called (because the shape of the ceiling suggests a cupcake paper), Angela

---

Facing page: Kaylee Harwood (Guenevere). Right: Guenevere enters from the stage right vomitorium.

Marshall, the other assistant stage manager, helps him return through the surprisingly vast maze of catwalks and lights suspended above the stage.

Arthur, who spends a lot of the musical consumed with self-doubt, comes up with an idea: a new society with noble ideals. "Might for right. That's it, Jenny! Not might is right. Might *for* right!"

Geraint Wyn Davies descends from the stage to one of the two vomitoriums located beneath the front rows. *Vomitorium*, from the Latin *vomere*, to spew, is the name given to the large openings at the base of amphitheatres that allowed large crowds to quickly exit. In the Festival Theatre they are the two passageways

The vomitoriums are used for downstage entrances and exits and quick costume changes

used for downstage entrances and exits and quick costume changes. Wyn Davies is dressed in armour, which has to be exchanged for a medieval gown in less than a minute. Four dressers and one wig person are on hand to do two fast changes with Wyn Davies and Carver. There is a wild flurry of activity as the plastic armour is discarded, and in less than a minute, everyone is gone. It has the feel of a crime scene.

Up in the stage manager's booth, Cynthia Toushan (known to all as Cindy) has a bird's-eye view of the stage. It is her job to oversee the performance—to "call" it, in theatrical parlance—and to ensure that the vision established by the director, whose work is finished after opening night, is precisely maintained for the duration of the run. (The director in this case, Gary Griffin, is in Chicago, working on *Follies* for the Chicago Shakespeare Theater and contemplating *42nd Street*, which he is to direct for Stratford's sixtieth season.)

Above: Company member Marcus Nance. Facing page: Cynthia Toushan runs *Camelot* from the stage manager's booth.

The stage manager will make sure, for example, that actors don't start to change the pace of a scene, introduce new bits of business or rethink their interpretations of their roles.

On a small table in front of Toushan is a seven-hundred-page "bible" in a three-ring binder. On the left-hand pages are the text and the musical score; on the right, a diagram of the set with notations of every actor's "blocking" (their movements around the stage) and the props that are being used. Several monitors show Toushan the stage and the conductor in the loft above it, along with an infrared view that enables her to see the actors exiting when the stage is in total blackness. It's easy to become disoriented and perhaps take a wrong turn in the sudden dark; Toushan doesn't want the lights to come up when someone is still making an exit.

Her left hand is beating out the musical count, while her right follows the text, turns the pages and works the switches to talk to the lighting and sound crew and to her assistants. Her non-stop patter is—to an outsider—a confusing combination of precisely timed technical direction and casual conversation. "LX 140 and spot cue 81. Go. Sound cue 212. Go. So it's the Rapture on Friday. Cool. What time? Warning on the traveller [the name for a theatre curtain that opens and closes sideways]. Here comes the king. LX 188. Go. LX 190. Gates opening. Traveller opening. LX 192. Go. Is anyone standing near Dave? Can you smack him, please?"

Toushan has been in the theatre since the age of ten, first as a performer and then as a stage manager for the last thirty years, fifteen of them in Stratford. At the beginning of every season, getting the hundreds of moving parts to work perfectly in a production like *Camelot* is a complex and daunting task. But now, in its ninety-sixth performance, it is as automatic as driving a car, and Toushan does it while carrying on more than one conversation. If she sees anything that doesn't appear in her scrupulously annotated text—a prop mishandled, a line dropped, a light cue missed—she makes note of it for next time.

Director of Music Rick Fox conducts *Camelot* in the Festival Theatre's orchestra loft.

During the twenty-minute intermission, the students in the audience discuss whether Arthur is going to, like, totally die in Act II. They debate the merits of the music and the day off from school this outing represents. A teacher moves up and down the aisles issuing a command: "Turn your cellphones off. Not just to vibrate. *All* the way off."

Just before Act II begins, in the loft above the stage, the twenty-six-piece orchestra begins that familiar warm-up cacophony known to fans of musical theatre. The musicians are segregated by glass dividers, the French horns at the back, the trombones next, bassoon to the side, drums near the front. They wait for the cue from conductor Rick Fox, who is also the Festival's Director of Music.

Fox's work on *Camelot* started a year ago, at the point of casting. He advises on what kind of voice is needed for a musical in a large theatre. Then he works with the actors. "You get them in there and work with them at a piano, work through the song, teach the song, discuss all the different options about how to sing the song, technical stuff like where to breathe, how to phrase the song, what pace. Because there's a million ways to sing a song. With Ger [Wyn Davies], it was about finding a balance between how much of a song is spoken, and how much is sung."

Camelot's score was tailored slightly for the Stratford production. The original had a four-minute overture, which was typical of the era. "At first we cut down the overture quite a bit," Fox says, "but it still sounded old-fashioned. And it takes a while to get into the story. We ended up scrapping the overture entirely, and I wrote new music for the opening scene. I used some themes from the show but crafted it around the scene with the hawk. I wanted to have swirling music; we had some singers backstage to give it a magical feel."

"Stand by," Fox says to his musicians, standing in front of a monitor that shows the stage. His baton swoops and they launch into the music for Act II.

Love, of course, is complicated. Guenevere has fallen in love with Lancelot but remains faithful to her husband. Seeing an opportunity in the unconsummated affair between Lancelot and Guenevere, Arthur's illegitimate son Mordred accuses them of treason. Lancelot escapes, but Guenevere is found guilty and sentenced to be burned at the stake. Luckily, Lancelot (lit to be a knight in shining armour) arrives, saves Guenevere and whisks her off to France.

Jonathan Winsby, as Lancelot, comes in and is helped out of his armour. "Breathe," he tells himself breathlessly. The change is done in a rapid twenty-three seconds.

"A record," the dresser says.

Up in the lighting booth, which looks down at the stage, master electrician Alec Cooper is managing the 235 lighting cues. Cindy Toushan's voice comes through a speaker. When she says "Go," he presses a button marked Go. On his computer all the cues are lined up. The five hundred lights that are fixed above the audience can create an astounding variety of colors and effects. Some are obvious—the spotlights that linger on an actor's face—but some are so subtle they barely register. They are like individual notes in a symphony. There are a hundred colour changes in the show. With the advent of computers, lighting has become symphonically complex.

As the story nears its conclusion, the Round Table is in ruins, most of its knights dead; Guenevere has become a nun; and war has taken its toll on everyone. Arthur finds a stowaway named Tom of Warwick, whom he instructs to go back to England and tell its citizens of the chivalry and honour that were the brief shining moment of Camelot. The lights dim, and the crowd, as they say, goes wild. The schoolchildren have been won over, applauding enthusiastically. They all file out into the pleasant waning autumn. The stagehands immediately descend, wrenches in hand, to begin the next changeover.

By 5 p.m., new buses arrive, dozens of them; there are fifteen hundred schoolchildren coming to *Twelfth Night*. They juggle apples on the lawn, flirt and compare jeans while waiting for their tour of the theatre.

Shakespeare's language may be unfamiliar to them, but the students will recognize the tensions and themes in the play, which have endured for four centuries. *Twelfth Night* was written around 1600, when Elizabethan England was going through a transition from land-based medieval economy to modern merchant society. Sir Toby Belch (Brian Dennehy) is an unemployed boozy knight, a relic from the past. The new era is embodied by Malvolio (Tom Rooney), an efficient, crisply-tailored steward looking to get ahead. The students won't get the Elizabethan references, but these two archetypes are familiar: the party boy versus

Backstage during *Twelfth Night*, company member Victor Dolhai (costumed and made up to be a John Lennon look-alike) hams it up with the show's prop pizza.

Above left: Juan Chioran (Fabian in *Twelfth Night*). Top: Ben Carlson (Feste). Above right: Scenic carpenter Anthony Gentile under the Festival Theatre stage, with the lift that elevates Malvolio's cage through the trapdoor in the floor. Facing page: Head of Automation Ian Phillips (left) and Technical Director Andrew Mestern inspect *Twelfth Night*'s automated refrigerator.

the striver. In the play there are the sharp divisions that high school breeds, as well as the foiled romances. There is a class clown (in this case, the jester Feste, played by Ben Carlson), the confusion about identity and the underlying loneliness behind all the masks. The play's subtitle, *What You Will*, is the seventeenth-century equivalent to "whatever." There are even electric guitars. So it is a recognizable world.

There are contingency plans for every prop and every piece of automated scenery

The play, directed by the Festival's Artistic Director, Des McAnuff, is set in Illyria, which is less a geographic location (though it was an ancient region on the eastern coast of the Adriatic Sea) than a state of mind (another commonality with high school). When McAnuff first sat down with designer Debra Hanson, who did both the set and the costumes, they had to decide *what* state of mind it was. The central ideas revolve around identity and vanity. Hanson has the faces of the two twins, Viola and Sebastian, woven into the floor design, as if they are lost at sea. It is a subtle, almost subliminal effect.

Backstage, Brian Dennehy, Stephen Ouimette (who plays Sir Andrew Aguecheek) and Andrea Runge (Viola and her alter ego, Cesario) are rehearsing the fight scenes. They need to nail both the swordplay and the comic timing: at one point in the production, Sir Andrew inadvertently grasps Viola's breast—a shock to him, as she is disguised as Cesario, a man. They move at less than full speed, swinging the swords with some deliberation. After ten minutes of warm-up, they file off to get into costume.

The production contains all the visual energy that is a dramatic signature of McAnuff's work. Much of

the scenery in *Twelfth Night* is automated, presenting complex technical challenges. A suspended refrigerator has automated doors that open. An umbrella appears through a hole in the floor and opens up (a particularly tricky gag to achieve). A cage rises through the floor. There is a boat that glides, a golf cart, a giant angel.

For a hallucinatory scene in which Feste impersonates a curate, McAnuff wanted him to be nine feet tall. The production team first tried a library ladder and then used it as a model to build their own version. Feste wears a long gown that covers the ladder and appears from the outside to be opaque but is sufficiently translucent from within to allow actor Cara Ricketts (as Maria) to see her way as she pushes him around. Its many technical requirements make this a complicated production to stage (though less so than Stratford's 2010 production of *The Tempest*), but there are contingency plans for every prop and every piece of automated scenery: if the gates don't close, if the boat won't budge, if the umbrella fails to rise, if the golf cart stalls.

On stage, Ben Carlson as Feste plays an electric bass. (Carlson was trained as both a classical and jazz musician.) A band slowly forms around him. Though music plays a huge role in this production, there is no orchestra in the loft; the sound is a combination of taped music and actors playing instruments live on stage. Since there is no conductor, the onstage musicians wear discreet earphones through which they hear a "click track" that acts as a metronome to keep them in sync with the taped music and with each other.

Sara Topham, who plays Olivia, lingers backstage. "Are there any kids?" she asks.

"Fifteen hundred."

Kids add a certain honesty, a unique energy, but they can be both distracted and distracting. The theatre holds 1,826 people, so there is little ballast for all those adolescent hormones.

Stephen Ouimette, who first came to Stratford in one of those yellow buses as a student and is in his eighteenth season as an actor here, sits in the golf cart backstage. He is dressed in ludicrous 1920s-era golf

Top: Jaz Sealey (a Jimi Hendrix-like Curio in *Twelfth Night*). Above left: Andrea Runge (Viola). Above right: Cara Ricketts (Maria).

clothes. As Sir Andrew Aguecheek, he is a recognizable archetype to the fifteen hundred students: here is the seventeenth-century equivalent to the stoner sidekick.

Ouimette suddenly yells "Fore!" and guns the golf cart, which races onto the stage at alarming speed, immediately coming to a jarring stop upstage.

Assistant stage manager Marie Fewer looks upward. "What's that sound?" An unexpected high-pitched tone has suddenly become audible. A handful of people gather, trying to locate it and figure out what's causing it. When Sara Topham comes off stage, she says she can't hear it on stage. It could be an oxygen tank, someone says. By phone they canvas the front-of-house people to see if there are any patrons with oxygen tanks. A malfunctioning light? A hearing aid? Before it can be figured out, it stops, to everyone's relief.

On stage, Brian Dennehy's Toby Belch is abusing Stephen Ouimette's Aguecheek. On alternate days, Dennehy's Max abuses Ouimette's Sam in Harold Pinter's vicious, bleak, subversively funny *The Homecoming* at the Avon Theatre. Dennehy's successful film career (*The Belly of an Architect*, *Righteous Kill*) has been exceeded by a stage career that has brought him two Tony Awards (for *Death of a Salesman* and *Long Day's Journey Into Night*). At seventy-three, he remains an imposing figure, with his wide shoulders and hawkish face, and he brings a hint of menace to the drunken charm of Toby Belch. (In *The Homecoming*, his Max is all menace.)

Backstage, Juan Chioran (Fabian) is getting ready to go on.

"What kind of accent do you want this evening?" he jokingly asks Marie, the assistant stage manager.

"How about Texan?"

He tries a few lines in a George Bush-like drawl.

"Perfect," she says.

There are small black-and-white monitors backstage that show the action on stage. Watching them is reminiscent of watching well-intentioned but static CBC dramas from the 1960s. It is an interesting exercise to see the play unfold from the perspective of a single, unmoving camera and to see it from the audience. The

Brian Dennehy (Sir Toby Belch) with company member Aaron Krohn.

Above: Wigs and makeup crew member Lena G. Festoso and *Twelfth Night* wardrobe master William C. Kraft (right) prepare for an actor's quick costume change. Facing page: The. John Grey runs *Twelfth Night* from the stage manager's booth.

two experiences have almost nothing in common. The essence of live theatre is the bond between actors and audience: that visceral, participatory relationship. A simple video image provides the plot and dialogue but none of the drama. (It takes proper cinematography, with moving cameras, multiple angles and close-ups, to achieve that—as with the film of McAnuff's *Twelfth Night* that was released in March 2012.)

And this is why teachers bring their students from Baltimore or Timmins to see the plays. The Shakespeare they studied in class suddenly comes to life. That language, which had seemed dense and opaque on the page, is suddenly comprehensible, the characters recognizable. And what may not seem funny in the written text is brought home by live performance.

Members of the band wander backstage with their guitars, practising rock riffs. Meanwhile, up in the stage manager's booth, The. John Gray issues the lighting and sound cues. (Since no two Equity members can use the same professional name, Gray somewhat whimsically adopted "Theocrates" as his first name—and contracted it to "The."—in order to distinguish himself from the actor and playwright John Gray, who wrote *Billy Bishop Goes to War*.) "Downstage, automation cue," he says. "LX 206. Go. LX 208. Go. Warning. Blacks close LX 210."

There are nineteen switches above him, each controlling a separate cue light for the actors backstage. An actor waiting to come on may not be able to clearly hear the onstage dialogue, so small light bulbs in various locations behind the scenes provide visual cues instead. When the light goes on, the actor gets ready; when it's turned off, that's his cue to enter. Gray's hands are always moving, following the score, flipping switches; his commands deal with immediate cues and warn of what's to come. The closest equivalent is air traffic controller.

There are more than three hundred lighting cues in *Twelfth Night*. It isn't just the technical feat of designing, programming and executing the lighting each night that the stage manager has to ensure. The actors have to "hit their marks" as well: find the precise spots on stage where they will be properly illuminated. As a show gets further into its run, the actors sometimes drift out of their light—and if an actor's face is in shadow, he or she is more difficult to hear.

The link between sound and light is partly psychological and partly physical. Gray points to four large moving lights that hang from the ceiling in front of him. Because these lights get very hot, each has a small fan. Those fans make noise, a subtle white noise that is barely audible but that infringes on the actors nonetheless. It takes up some aural space. And the Festival Theatre, while intimate for its size, is still a large space for actors to speak in without a microphone.

When the cue light goes on, the actor gets ready; when it's turned off, that's his cue to enter

Below him, Dennehy, Ouimette and Chioran are in purple towels and bathrobes. The trap in the centre of the set is open, issuing steam. As Ouimette parades around the stage, his towel suddenly comes undone, providing a quick glimpse of his derrière. He quickly grasps the towel and re-tucks it. The audience gasps, not entirely sure if that was meant to happen. In fact, it is a prop towel devised by Ouimette and the wardrobe people. When Ouimette heard that McAnuff wanted the characters onstage in towels with nothing underneath, he proposed going one step further. The towel is taped in such a way that it won't fall all the way off, revealing the same glimpse for each performance.

When the tennis net is set up for Malvolio's "yellow stockings" scene, stools are placed downstage, near the edge. They are to sit on, but also, more critically, to mark the edge of the stage when Sara Topham is backing up

during the scene, chased by Malvolio, who is dressed as an Elizabethan idiot, convinced that his employer, Olivia, is in love with him. This is another trope familiar to many students in the audience: making a fool of yourself for love, or what feels like love at the time.

Debra Hanson designed the beginning of the play to have an almost Victorian darkness. Splashes of colour are introduced (the golf clothes and Malvolio's Elizabethan costume), finally giving way to the happy cream colours of the finale. From darkness to light, though not *all* is light.

This is another trope familiar to many students in the audience: making a fool of yourself for love

In the end, Malvolio is revealed as a conceited ass, Aguecheek remains alone and dim, and Sir Toby is still a man out of time. There are several happy endings, and love is everywhere, but it has left in its wake bruised egos, diminished reputations and a sense of vulnerability and loneliness: themes that sit in the hearts of half the audience. They file out and into the waiting buses, counted dutifully by teachers and chaperones, ready to sleep in their seats and dream of love as the bus hurtles back to Oklahoma or Sudbury.

The fifty-ninth season of the Stratford Shakespeare Festival is almost wrapped. In a few days, the buses will cease, and the theatres will darken until spring, when *MacHomer*, *Much Ado About Nothing*, *42nd Street*, *You're a Good Man, Charlie Brown*, *Cymbeline*, *The Pirates of Penzance* and *The Matchmaker* all arrive on stage, the first wave in a total of fourteen productions to be mounted in 2012. Hundreds of workers are done for the season. But hundreds remain, preparing, sketching, marketing, experimenting, worrying and dreaming about the next season.

Facing page: Part of designer Debra Hanson's set for *Twelfth Night*. Above: Sara Topham (Olivia).

Left: Andrea Runge (Viola in *Twelfth Night*, here shown in her disguise as "Cesario"). Right: Lucy Peacock's dressing table. Facing page: The *Twelfth Night* curtain call as seen from the stage left vomitorium.

Notes and Asides:

Shakespeare and the School Bus

Many people's first encounter with Shakespeare on stage comes from visiting Stratford on a yellow school bus. In 1958, Stratford's first year of student matinées, more than fifty-six hundred students attended six performances; today, over sixty thousand attend annually. (The millionth student passed through the Festival's doors on October 9, 1976.) But as the classics quietly disappear from school curricula, will the buses keep coming?

"When I was a student," says Artistic Director Des McAnuff, "I studied plays such as *Henry IV, Part 1* and *Twelfth Night*—titles that are no longer on the curriculum. Focus has narrowed in our schools to just four or five big titles, and if our playbill doesn't happen to include one of those, we will see our school attendance drop dramatically. Clearly, we need to find creative ways of helping teachers open up much wider theatrical vistas to their students."

That task falls to the Festival's Education Department, which began in 1977 with a staff of one, a bi-annual newsletter for students and a few visits to local schools. Embracing a mission first articulated by the Festival's founders—"to promote interest in and the study of the arts generally, and literature, drama and music in particular and to advance knowledge and appreciation of and to stimulate interest in Shakespearean culture and tradition"—it has since grown into one of the most comprehensive and far-reaching facilities for teaching Shakespeare in the world.

Teaching Shakespeare used to involve memorizing soliloquies, which deadened the text rather than bringing it to life. "Getting teachers to be more daring and relaxed with Shakespeare, getting them to lose that sense of reverence, is critically important," says the Festival's General Director, Antoni Cimolino. "When a play is up on its feet, kids love it."

The Festival's flagship Teaching Shakespeare Program, which helps educators develop creative classroom techniques, has grown from twelve classes of

Facing page: Company member Barbara Fulton leads students in the Shakespeare on Wheels program. Right: Company member Mike Shara (centre) in a Prologue.

local teachers and their students to more than a hundred classes coming from as far away as Sudbury, Kenora and St. John. Most schools within an hour and a half radius of Stratford have been visited by Shakespeare on Wheels, a program in which a director, designer, musician and choreographer work with students to mount a scene from a Shakespeare play in their own school. And the Ontario Schools Project serves an additional four thousand students and their teachers through curriculum-based lesson packages, artist support in the classroom, and ticket and transportation subsidies. Its ultimate aim is to give every student in Ontario the opportunity to get to Stratford at least once in his or her educational career.

"Through Shakespeare, kids can be taught to understand creative concepts that prepare them for life"

"This is one of the most vital investments we can make, not just for ourselves but for our entire society," says Des McAnuff. "Through Shakespeare, kids can be taught to understand creative concepts and to absorb the narrative complexity that will prepare them for the complexity of life."

Besides these three core programs, the department provides schools with more than 150 ad hoc opportunities each year, including private workshops, tours and talk-back sessions, and sends artists to work with students as far afield as Michigan. It also offers, under the rubric Beyond the Stage, nearly a hundred events and activities for the general public.

"Looking back on the sixty years of the Festival's history," says Andrea Jackson, the Festival's Director of Education, "one of the key elements of our success has been our long-term commitment to enriching the experiences not just of students and teachers but of everyone who comes to our theatres. It's through our education programs that we build an engaged and loyal audience today, and an increasingly knowledgeable one in the future."

Company member Sean Arbuckle with students in a Prologue.

Chapter Two

A Delicate Balance: Planning the Playbill

To mount a play in Shakespeare's London it was necessary to overcome the government's suspicion of theatres (places for the plague and subversives to gather), censorship and a troubled economy that was stretched to support England's naval ambitions. Theatre companies had to deal with the public appetite for cruder, cheaper and more visceral entertainment (bear-baitings, hangings and floggings). And there were the usual mishaps once a production was actually mounted. (The Globe theatre burned down in 1613 during a performance of *Henry VIII* when a cannon used to mark the king's entrance set fire to the thatched roof.)

A version of this remains today. The government has limited resources for the arts, and people continue to flock to cruder amusements, which are much more plentiful now and only slightly less crude. And Shakespeare is four hundred years older than he was.

So a question arises each season, often unstated, but not always: Why do Shakespeare? The standard answer is that he is our greatest playwright. But equally important is the fact that he is still relevant. Perhaps increasingly relevant. What bureaucrat hasn't recognized Iago among his colleagues? What political intrigue doesn't evoke one of Shakespeare's histories? We saw versions of Richard III in Saddam Hussein and Moammar Gadhafi. There are echoes of Macbeth on Bay and Wall streets. We've seen Hamlet (Michael Ignatieff's political run) and a hint of Lear (Conrad Black). Shakespeare's characters remain as vivid as they were four centuries ago.

But it isn't their villainy or nobility that makes them interesting; it is their ambiguity. How do we view Hamlet: righteous avenger or serial killer? Is Henry V a hero or a war criminal? We don't get many clues from Shakespeare, whose own views remain aloof. Was he Catholic? Gay? Was he an anti-Semitic careerist adulterer? Whoever and whatever he was has been distilled to his work.

He keeps our attention, in part, because he isn't static. Actors who play Hamlet or Lear or Macbeth more than once in their career rarely play him the same way. Directors don't approach the play in the same way twice, because they have changed in the interim and the text now resonates in new ways.

Deciding which of Shakespeare's plays to stage each season starts with Des McAnuff

"I have directed *Macbeth* three times," says Artistic Director Des McAnuff. "In each case, I saw the play in very different terms. The first time, I saw it in terms of the Kennedy assassination. Having lived through that as a kid, I could understand the devastating consequences of a country's wound that won't heal. The second time was before I'd become a father. Then I saw the play as very much about a childless couple. I understood how a career could become a substitute for a child. It was only in the 2009 production at Stratford that I felt I came close to a balanced, holistic sense of the play—seeing not just the whole but all of the nooks and crannies that had eluded me before."

Deciding which of Shakespeare's almost forty plays to stage each season starts with McAnuff, whose job it is to set the playbill. He became Stratford's Artistic Director in 2007, when he shared the role with Don Shipley and

Artistic Director Des McAnuff in rehearsal for his production of *Jesus Christ Superstar* (2011).

Marti Maraden, then took over the following year as sole director. For seventeen years he was Artistic Director of La Jolla Playhouse in California; his two tenures there (from 1983 to 1994 and again from 2001 to 2007) saw the theatre win more than three hundred awards, including twenty-eight Tonys. McAnuff himself has won two Tonys for directing—for *Big River* and for *The Who's Tommy*, which he also co-wrote—and has received many awards and nominations for his other productions, including the global hit *Jersey Boys*.

"The most important element in planning a season has to do with the artists"

"With a classical repertory company," he says, "we have to play close attention to our own history. We have to ensure that we don't let any part of the Shakespearean canon become unduly neglected. Equally, we don't want to do *Henry V* five times within a single decade. So when we're planning a season, we have to think about what we've done in the recent past."

Henry V is the Shakespeare play that McAnuff chose to direct for the sixtieth season, while General Director Antoni Cimolino took on *Cymbeline*. *Cymbeline* has been produced only three times before at Stratford (most recently in 2004), and *Henry V* was last done in 2001. The latter has been described by some critics as among Shakespeare's "problem plays," a term that McAnuff feels has more to do with the interpreters than with the plays themselves. To round out the Shakespeare program, McAnuff decided on a comedy, *Much Ado About Nothing*. There needs to be balance. Everything can't be as violent as *Titus Andronicus*. You can't do all comedies, or all romances.

Choosing which Shakespeare plays to do involves a lot of consultation. McAnuff talks both to Cimolino and to Festival Dramaturge Robert Blacker. The choice of *Cymbeline*, for instance, arose from a discussion about which of Shakespeare's "late romances"—four thematically and stylistically related works that he wrote toward the end of his career—might be performed. Two of those plays, *The Tempest* (with Christopher Plummer) and *The Winter's Tale*, had been done in 2010, so that narrowed the options to *Cymbeline* or *Pericles*.

The initial meetings, which take place eighteen months before the season opens, also include Associate Artistic Director Dean Gabourie, Executive Producer Judith Richardson and Casting Director Beth Russell. A host of factors go into their choices. Are they exciting? Do they resonate culturally? Are they financially viable? And—most critically—who will direct and who will play the parts?

"The most important element that goes into planning a season," McAnuff says, "has to do with the artists. There are two huge dynamics here. One has to do with our company of actors. It ebbs and flows: people go off and do other things, others return, and all the while we are creating a new generation of actors through the Birmingham Conservatory for Classical Theatre [the Festival's in-house training program] to replenish the company. So as Artistic Director I am very mindful of the troops: our leading players and the company at large. It is critical that they continue to be challenged and that we showcase their extraordinary talents.

"The other, equally important dynamic is that at the helm of each production is an artist who has a vision for the work. Most often that's the director, whether it's a visiting artist like Adrian Noble or one of our Canadian colleagues like Marti Maraden or Jennifer Tarver or Chris Abraham. With contemporary repertoire, it can be a playwright like Morris Panych or Michel Tremblay. Or it could be an actor. In 2012, Christopher Plummer is doing his one-man show *A Word or Two*, and that is very much his vision as both the actor and the creator of the piece."

Because the planning happens so far in advance, it means the Festival is always operating on three planes:

Facing page: Artistic Director Des McAnuff with Christopher Plummer (Prospero) in rehearsal for *The Tempest* (2010). Above: Director Jennifer Tarver in rehearsal for *The Homecoming* (2011).

Above: Director Chris Abraham in rehearsal for *The Little Years* (2011). Facing page: General Director Antoni Cimolino in rehearsal for his production of *Bartholomew Fair* (2009).

the current season, the upcoming season and the season after that.

Much of the task of keeping these balls in the air falls to Antoni Cimolino. He is an unlikely General Director in some ways, reminiscent of the *New Yorker* cartoon in which a man at a desk says, "I used to be an actor but I got bit by the accounting bug." It was as an actor that Cimolino first came to the Festival in 1988; four seasons later, he played Romeo to Megan Follows's Juliet.

"However," he says, "as time went on, I realized that my imagination was now being pulled towards the construction of the whole: trying to work with others towards creating theatre. So there was a movement away from the subjectivity of 'I am a colour in the canvas' to 'Where should the colour go in the canvas? What colour should it be?'" His interest shifted to directing, then grew to encompass aspects of the theatre outside the rehearsal hall.

Now, as General Director, he is involved in fundraising, marketing and plotting the future of the Festival, both physically (the construction of the Studio Theatre, the renovation of the Avon) and financially. He has always, however, kept one foot firmly in the artistic camp. At Stratford, he has won acclaim for directing such productions as 2009's *Bartholomew Fair* and the 2011 season's *The Grapes of Wrath*; his work elsewhere includes the Canadian première of *Enron*, which sold out its run in Calgary in February 2012.

It is unusual in the theatre world to have an artist in this position of fiscal responsibility, though Cimolino considers the image of artists as dreamy and financially naive to be a misperception. "There is this idea that artists can't count," he says. "But Michelangelo knew exactly how much to overcharge the Pope for the Sistine Chapel." There is an old story about a woman asking Picasso what artists talked about in those cafés, and Picasso answering, "We talk about the cost of turpentine." There is a certain practicality to art, Cimolino says, and there always has been. "Shakespeare himself was a shareholder. He was busy running the company, and the company made them all rich."

Balancing the artistic and the financial sides of the Festival is a delicate task. Less than four percent of the $60-million budget comes from government grants. The rest comes from private donations and box-office sales. Cimolino needs to help McAnuff shape a season that is artistically engaging and will also pay the bills. His expertise in both the administrative and artistic sides of the Festival has stood him in good stead in that regard and made him the prime candidate in the search for a successor when McAnuff's tenure ends. Few were surprised, therefore, when it was announced that at the conclusion of the 2012 season Cimolino would become the Festival's next Artistic Director.

Balancing the agendas of different departments in compiling the master schedule is like solving a Rubik's Cube

In addition to Shakespeare and the classics, the Festival is increasingly committed to new work. "Shakespeare richly deserves his place at the centre of our dramatic universe," McAnuff says. "But our founders also made a wise decision when they were planning their second season in 1954: not to do *only* Shakespeare. While Shakespeare occupies centre stage here, it's important that we see him in the context of his contemporaries and also that he be able to rub shoulders with those who preceded him and those who have inherited his dramatic genes. To fully appreciate him, we have to surround him with other great classics and with the best in new writing."

Planning those other works involves many factors. "Ideally," says Cimolino, "you need a playbill that's irresistible to the audience, appropriate for your artists and financially prudent." Whatever choices are made, inevitably they create complications within the company. "If it's good for the technical director," Cimolino says, "then it's managed to upset the stage manager. If it's good for the actors, it doesn't work for the sewers. There are these tensions, and you always have to have a balance, and the same is true in putting a season together."

The word *balance* also springs to the lips of Jason Miller, the Festival's Creative Planning Director. As part of a team that also includes Executive Producer Judith Richardson, Producer David Auster and Assistant Producer Bonnie Green (who, among other things, are responsible for negotiating rights and contracts, and for finding ways to realize artistic visions within the allotted budget), Miller has the task of drawing up the master schedule: a massive document that details everything that will happen at the Festival over the coming year.

"The master schedule answers all the 'w' questions for the artists," says Miller: "who's working together, which plays they're assigned to, where they're scheduled to rehearse or create, and when they need to complete their tasks."

In compiling it, Miller has to balance at least six different agendas, from the Production Department's construction timelines to the Marketing Department's need to offer patrons the greatest possible variety of performances throughout the season. "It's like solving a Rubik's Cube," he says, adding that his approach to the task can be summed up in a six-word motto: "Anything is possible—just not *everything*."

One constant in every season is musical theatre, which has a long tradition at Stratford. Tyrone Guthrie himself directed the Festival's first full-blown musical, Gilbert and Sullivan's *HMS Pinafore*, in 1960 and followed it up with *The Pirates of Penzance* in 1961, the year that G&S operettas entered the public domain, allowing for more artistic freedom in their staging.

"We know we'll do musicals," Cimolino says. "The question is which ones, and how will they work with the rest of the repertoire." Nowadays there are usually

Facing page: Creative Planning Director Jason Miller. Above: Gareth Potter (Henry, Earl of Richmond) with director Miles Potter in rehearsal for *Richard III* (2011).

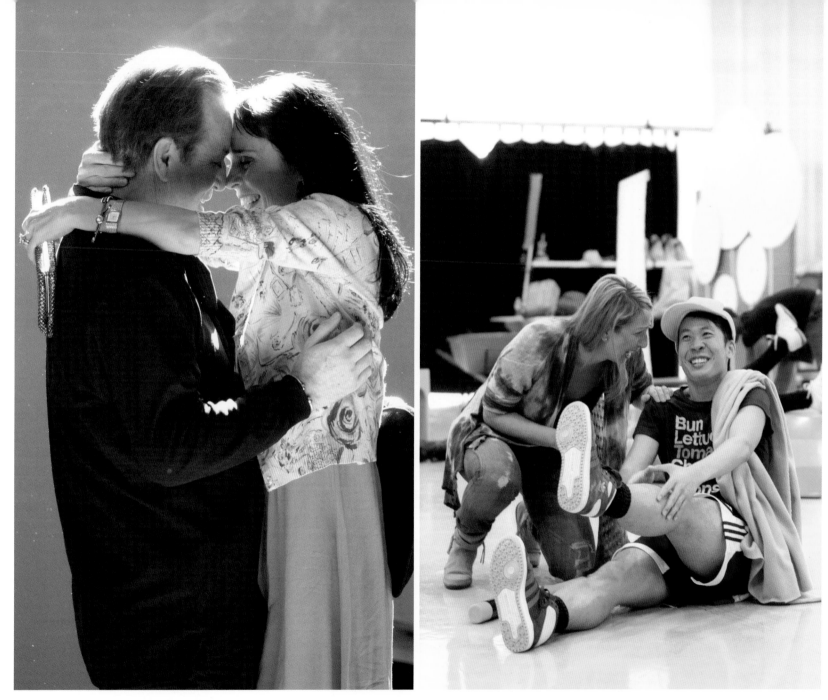

Facing page: Director Gary Griffin in rehearsal for *Camelot*. Above left: C. David Johnson (Pat Denning) and Cynthia Dale (Dorothy Brock) in rehearsal for *42nd Street* (2012). Above right: Director Donna Feore and Kevin Yee (Linus) in rehearsal for *You're a Good Man, Charlie Brown* (2012).

two musicals per season, though the 2012 season has four. In addition to *The Pirates of Penzance* and *42nd Street*, *You're a Good Man, Charlie Brown* was chosen as a family show, a recurring feature at Stratford. *Wanderlust*, a world première commissioned by the Festival, continues Stratford's relationship with Canadian playwright Morris Panych. It was Panych who chose to write a musical this time around. With Marek Norman as composer, it's inspired by the life and works of Canada's famed "Bard of the Yukon," Robert W. Service.

Another consideration in choosing repertoire is the need to consciously build an audience for the future. *Jesus Christ Superstar* is a musical that straddles certain demographics, appealing first to boomers who may have owned the original 1970 recording or who remember seeing Norman Jewison's film. But both the music and Des McAnuff's 2011 production appealed to a younger audience as well. The result was a huge hit that went to La Jolla and then to Broadway, where it opened at the Neil Simon Theatre in March 2012.

The audience is always a factor in determining the playbill. "I want to have a series of dramatic journeys for the audience to go on," says McAnuff, "so I am constantly thinking of where we want to lead the audience. That may have to do with a reflection of the times we live in, or it may have to do with suggesting *changes* for the times we live in. I think we have a responsibility to effect change when we can. An excellent example is *King of Thieves*, a new musical we premièred in 2010 that grew out of these terrible economic times. Its author, George F. Walker, had a strong view of the contemporary banking system. I think he wanted to plug into *The Beggar's Opera* and *The Threepenny Opera* and be part of that tradition of playwriting, to be backed up by those classics as he took on our own time."

In choosing *The Grapes of Wrath*, which Antoni Cimolino directed in 2011, there was a recognition of how topical the themes were. Steinbeck's Dust Bowl Okies held parallels to 2008's subprime mortgage victims. McAnuff brought the show to Cimolino in the

Facing page: General Director Antoni Cimolino with Gregor Reynolds (Winfield) and Abigail Winter-Culliford (Ruthie) in rehearsal for his production of *The Grapes of Wrath* (2011). Above: Artistic Director Des McAnuff in rehearsal for his production of *Twelfth Night* (2011).

Top, from left: Daniel McIvor (Hamilton), director Dean Gabourie, John Beale (Kyle) and dramaturge Iris Turcott with Buddy T. Dog rehearse MacIvor's play *The Best Brothers* (2012). Above left: Director Darko Tresnjak in rehearsal for *Titus Andronicus* (2011). Above right: Director Donna Feore in rehearsal with the cast of *You're a Good Man, Charlie Brown* (2012). Facing page: Jennifer Rider-Shaw (Peggy Sawyer) and Stephen Cota (Frankie) in rehearsal for *42nd Street* (2012).

Above: General Director Antoni Cimolino with, from left, Jon de Leon (Cutting) and Michael Spencer-Davis (Bristle) in rehearsal for *Bartholomew Fair* (2009). Facing page: Stage manager Bona Duncan and director Christopher Newton in rehearsal for *Much Ado About Nothing* (2012).

summer of 2009, just after the economic meltdown. "I read it," says Cimolino, "and thought it had a very powerful message for people today. It's what happens to you when everything that protects and comforts you has been stripped away."

The result of all that debate, artistic vision, and juggling of schedules, cast and genres is usually an eclectic mix of titles, and the 2012 season is no exception.

"We wanted something that's exciting and touches as many people as possible"

The Festival's two leaders are each directing a Shakespeare play, while another, *Much Ado About Nothing*, is being directed by Christopher Newton, who acted at Stratford before serving for many years as Artistic Director of the Shaw Festival. Christopher Plummer, perhaps the most famous of Stratford's senior artists, has his one-man show *A Word or Two*.

There is the new (*The Best Brothers*, by Daniel McIvor, and *Wanderlust*), the ancient (*Elektra*) and the reinvented (*MacHomer*, a version of *Macbeth* performed in the voices of fifty *Simpsons* characters by actor and comedian Rick Miller).

There is something for the kids (*You're a Good Man, Charlie Brown*), for history buffs (*The War of 1812*), for Stratford aficionados (*Hirsch*, chronicling the life of former Artistic Director John Hirsch). There is the long-awaited return of Gilbert and Sullivan (*The Pirates of Penzance*), as well as classic Broadway (*42nd Street*, *The Matchmaker*).

"Ultimately, we wanted something that's exciting and touches as many people as possible," Cimolino says.

New Plays in a Classical Context

A dramaturge's role in working with a playwright combines psychiatrist, best friend and nagging parent"

When Des McAnuff became Stratford's Artistic Director, new Canadian plays were among his top priorities. He saw them as a natural complement to a classical repertoire.

"New texts continually spring into being," he says, "in direct artistic response to the experiences of today. They're new, but not unconnected to what has gone before. The DNA of the classics invariably transmits itself into our new stories, our new forms, our new ideas. In a living theatrical tradition, the past is always prologue, and the present is always our entry into the past. That is why it is important to present new work side by side with classics. We should find resonance between the past and the present—using the words of the former to shed light on the latter."

Shakespeare's plays were, of course, new in their time. Until the Elizabethan era, most London theatre had been either Tudor morality plays or works taken from the Greek and Roman canons. But Shakespeare and Marlowe and Jonson launched a new tradition, one that saw recent history or current events being depicted on stage. Shakespeare's genius was that he was able to make those events both universal and timeless. The theatre became an enormously popular pastime; on a given afternoon, ten percent of London's population could be found in a theatre. They revelled in this reflection of their world. Some of Shakespeare's work was, in the context of the day, radical.

Thirty years ago, producing Canadian plays was seen as radical. To assist in the development of new work at Stratford, McAnuff hired Bob White as the Consulting Director of New Plays. "When I first started in the business," White says, "and when my generation first started lobbying for the production and development of new Canadian plays, there was no such thing as a Canadian playwright. But over the last twenty-five years practically every theatre in the country has done new work, and Canadian playwrights are produced all the time. It's a revolution that was won."

White works closely with Festival Dramaturge Robert Blacker, and they often alternate in shepherding new plays to fruition. Their role in working with a playwright, says White, "combines psychiatrist, best friend and nagging parent: all the different kinds of relationships you can have with a writer to move the script along."

Under McAnuff, the Festival has taken a tripartite approach to Canadian drama. In the first place, it has commissioned new work from such prominent playwrights as Morris Panych, Judith Thompson and John Mighton. Stratford has also been revisiting the canon of what might be called Canadian classics—in particular, by reviving two renowned dramas from the 1970s: George F. Walker's *Zastrozzi* and Michel Tremblay's *Hosanna*. The third component of its strategy has been to facilitate the writing and development of new work by Canadian writers. To that end, Blacker started the Playwrights Retreat in 2007.

"We try and have a group of eight playwrights who are very diverse," White says, "both culturally and where they are in their careers: senior writers, mid-career, early career. We have such a big country that writers rarely have the opportunity to exchange experiences, especially in a situation that isn't complicated by ordinary life."

Facing page: Playwright Andrew Moodie (left) and Bob White, Consulting Director, New Plays. Right: Araya Mengesha as Tommy in Sunil Kuruvilla's *Rice Boy* (2009).

Chapter Three

The Aesthetic Field Marshal: The Role of the Director

The role of director has evolved over the centuries. In ancient Greek theatre, it was the *choragus* who directed the song and movement on stage, and it was the playwright himself who likely cast and staged the production. A director isn't listed for the earliest productions of Shakespeare; it wasn't till the eighteenth century that the role began to take shape, and not till the twentieth that the director assumed some of the qualities of *auteur*.

Stratford's first director—and first Artistic Director—was Tyrone Guthrie. He was a legend before he came to Stratford, having revived the idea of classical theatre in England after a relatively fallow period. (The appeal of Shakespeare has been nearly universal but it hasn't always been constant.) With his considerable height (six foot six) and strong features, Guthrie was an imposing figure. William Shatner once recalled how, when Guthrie descended the steep rake of the original outdoor theatre at Stratford, a ray of light coming in from a flap in the tent, it was easy to mistake him for God.

"Tyrone was a magical man," Christopher Plummer once recalled in an interview with fellow actor R.H. Thompson. "As a director, he was a thousand people. He sat there and laughed, cried and encouraged you to do your utmost. You came to work for him as if you were in front of a thousand people." Plummer said that Guthrie viewed theatre as a combination of religion and the circus. "He had lovely, original ideas of how to keep Shakespeare alive in the contemporary world. He was an innovator and a leader. He gave you raw,

new looks at Shakespeare. He was an extraordinary, extraordinary man."

In the modern era, each director defines the job for himself. But he or she usually takes the lead in every aspect of the production, from casting to design to music.

Des McAnuff believes that the most critical ingredient for a director is passion. "It is very important that you have something in your heart that needs to explode when you take on a play," he says. "A friend of mine—a director named JoAnne Akalaitis—describes the role of the director as a kind of aesthetic field marshal. I think that is a terrific description."

Passion is one of the criteria that McAnuff uses when setting a season's playbill. He canvasses directors he knows and admires, and asks them what it is they are dying to do. "The best projects are artist-driven," he says. "I turn to the passions of others." It is also an essential criterion for the plays he chooses to direct himself, such as 2010's production of *The Tempest*.

"I was interested in that play for a long time," he says. "I was probably drawn to it for very personal reasons: I have had more than one home during my life, and I think I understand something about the spirit of banishment and isolation and returning home. Other plays that have drawn me—*Macbeth*, for example—probably had a lot to do with being a Canadian, growing up in a former colony and trying to bring that experience to one of Shakespeare's texts."

The first step in staging any Shakespeare play is to read the complete text. But what constitutes the original text in Shakespeare? Many of his plays come to us in multiple versions. About half of them were published individually in various editions (known as quartos) during the playwright's lifetime; then in 1623 John Heminges and Henry Condell published the first collected edition of Shakespeare's works: the First Folio. There are differences between these versions because copy could come from the playwright's original manuscript

Director Weyni Mengesha with Gareth Potter in rehearsal for *Hosanna* (2011).

60

Christopher Plummer and Des McAnuff with host George Stroumboulopoulos on CBC TV's *The Hour*.

(Shakespeare's "foul papers") or the prompt book keeper's record of a performance, usually with cuts and other changes, and thus shorter. So "the complete original text" often really means some version of these from a quarto text or the Folio or a conflation of the two.

"Text analysis is a moving target," McAnuff says. "Even plays we've done in the past, we go back to." *Henry V*, a play in which Shakespeare examines the nature of leadership, is one that McAnuff has always wanted to direct. The culmination of an eight-play cycle on English history, it comes to roughly the same conclusion that Machiavelli did in *The Prince* (translations of which became available in England about ten years before Shakespeare began his histories): it isn't always the nicest person who makes the best leader.

"The first pass," says McAnuff, "is mainly to identify cuts: *Henry V* is a very long play, and we had to do some sensitive pruning." The task of trimming the

play for performance often falls to the dramaturge, an unseen and generally poorly understood position in the theatre. A dramaturge's duties are principally related to script. In the case of new plays, that usually involves working with director and playwright, helping to realize their intentions. With a script that is four centuries old, it's more about trying to see through the layers of other people's past interpretations to form your own view of the playwright's intentions, so you can make your cuts accordingly.

Stratford's supervising Dramaturge is Robert Blacker. "In some ways it's a terrifying experience," he says of the task of cutting *Henry V*. "The author is not here to answer questions." Blacker was aided by the extensive Festival Archives, which houses information about all of Stratford's past productions. For *Henry V*, it was possible to get a colour-coded version of the script that showed the cuts that had been made by various directors over the years.

"People form opinions about Shakespeare plays based on productions in which the scripts have been cut down," he says, "so it is important to read his plays in their entirety to understand what Shakespeare is really trying to do. For example, there are many scenes in *Romeo and Juliet* that are seldom seen on stage. Most productions focus only on the love story and cut as much as a fifth of the text in scenes that deal with what Shakespeare called 'the continuance of their parents' rage.' Why did Shakespeare write them? One way to answer that question is to find out what was going on England at the time Shakespeare was writing the play."

In *Romeo and Juliet* (as well as *Twelfth Night*), Blacker explains, you see the land-based medieval economy giving way to the new merchant economy of the modern world. "This leads us to see the Montagues and the Capulets as Old Money and New Money," he says, "and so the competition between them takes on a familiar edge. It's all about bringing the text closer to the audience. Money is important in the play. When Romeo buys poison to kill himself, he pays the Apothecary with these words: 'There is thy gold, worse poison to men's souls . . . than these poor compounds.'

"With *Henry V*," says Blacker, "people are still affected by Laurence Olivier's film version, which came out during the Second World War and was designed to rally the country." It would be easy to suppose that in its own time Shakespeare's play reflected a sublimated public yearning for a forceful leader—Queen Elizabeth was aging, and Henry was remembered as forever young (as a result of his early death) and a great warrior—but Shakespeare takes this potent and seductive icon and gives us a Henry who is far more complex.

It's not just the director and the dramaturge who contribute to this process, Blacker points out. Designers and actors bring their intelligence and intuition to the process. New ideas are discovered in rehearsal. "I like working with Des because he will take the best idea in the room," Blacker says. "By 'best idea' I mean the most profound understanding of the script, because ultimately it's about serving the writer. The

Top: General Director Antoni Cimolino at the first rehearsal for his production of *Cymbeline* (2012). Above left: Dramaturge Robert Blacker: Above right: Director Frank Galati with Andrew Gillies in rehearsal for *The Merry Wives of Windsor* (2011).

Developing the Directors of the Future

It was Michael Langham, Artistic Director from 1956 to 1967, who first articulated the secret of directing on a thrust stage. "He imagined two proscenium arches intersecting diagonally across the stage," says Associate Artistic Director Dean Gabourie. "Once you see it that way, you understand how the thrust stage works."

That's just one of the insights offered by the Festival's Michael Langham Workshop for Classical Direction. Designed by Gabourie and Theatre Training Consultant David Latham, and coordinated by Assistant Producer Bonnie Green, the two-year program enables emerging Canadian directors, a dozen of whom are chosen from some ninety applicants each year, to gain experience working with the classics on a large scale.

"They become familiar with every aspect of this institution, from fundraising to the astounding wealth of material in our Archives," says Gabourie. "They assist the directors of our productions and work with other renowned directors whom we bring in from outside." The program culminates in the fall with an in-house presentation of scenes from the classical repertoire, using Festival actors. "Participants stay in contact once they leave, so we're building a network of artistic connections across the country, which ultimately benefits us all."

Participants in the 2011 Langham Workshop. Back row, from left: Rachel Slaven, Andrew Shaver, Eric Benson, Sharon Bajer, Heather Davies, Associate Artistic Director Dean Gabourie, Alan Dilworth, Jarrick Grimes and Lezlie Wade. Front row: Dian Marie Bridge, Artistic Director Des McAnuff, Rachel Peake and Thomas Morgan Jones.

choices Des makes helps the audience understand what is going on in the text."

Blacker first grasped Shakespeare's political relevance during McAnuff's 1981 staging of *Henry IV* for New York's Shakespeare in the Park. "This was following Nixon's presidency," he says, "and we realized that the Earl of Worcester was a version of Nixon's Secretary of War, Alexander Haig. I understood that Shakespeare *isn't* four hundred years old. He stands the test of time because he was so astute in his understanding of both individuals and institutions. To see the character of Henry V in his full complexity is an extraordinary experience. In his history plays, Shakespeare examines political systems that are still with us today."

Certainly, *Henry V* has political and military themes that resonate in our times. But how far do you push that analogy? Do you situate Henry in Afghanistan, for example?

"There's no recipe," McAnuff says. "Sometimes it's tempting to make a statement, but I'm more interested in larger resonances. I first directed *Henry IV, Part 1* when Jimmy Carter was leaving office and Ronald Reagan was coming in. You couldn't help but feel that parallel in the play. And I think that's the best use, maybe. So with *Henry V*, there are many ideas that have a contemporary reference. One thinks of Stephen Harper or Barack Obama—a look at the nature of leadership.

"The most dangerous thing about *Henry V* is deciding that it's an anti-war play—or that Hal needs to be a hero, so you need to take a patriotic approach. Shakespeare embraced paradox, and both those ideas are in *Henry V*. It's hard to eliminate one point of view; you need them both. So ultimately I'm comfortable with the play's historicism. My production looks like what we imagine the fifteenth century looks like. The parallels will be there anyway."

While the text is the most important aspect to McAnuff, his productions have a distinctive visual energy, and he has embraced the use of automation in his productions, from the various devices in *Twelfth*

Night to an automated drawbridge in *Henry V*. "It's liberating," he says. "The dramatic architecture in Shakespeare's work is breathtaking, and when you can keep up with that by using contemporary stagecraft, it's liberating. We are, at our core, a language-based theatre, but you also want to stimulate the audience visually. But the main thing is the talent of the actors."

"People form opinions about Shakespeare plays based on productions in which the scripts have been cut down"

Having a large repertory company makes casting both a luxury and a challenge. "The cross-casting is like a three-dimensional chess game," McAnuff says. It's a challenge to cast an entire season that has actors in multiple roles; the logistics are complex and daunting. And a dozen actors were interested in playing Henry. "We had auditions for Hal," McAnuff says. The result was that Aaron Krohn, who made his Stratford debut in 2011 as Lenny in *The Homecoming*, won the role.

One of the advantages of Stratford's extraordinary pool of actors is that you get major talents playing smaller parts that often complement larger parts in other productions. "What that does," McAnuff says, "is create 'bench strength'—to use a sports analogy. You have these great actors in smaller roles."

Antoni Cimolino was drawn to directing *Cymbeline* for the 2012 season in part because of where he was in his own life: the play is about fathers and their children, and he has a grown son and daughter.

"Every parent has moments they'd like to take back,

Director Brian Bedford (right) with Stephen Ouimette (Canon Chasuble) in rehearsal for *The Importance of Being Earnest* (2009).

Christopher Plummer (Prospero) with director Des McAnuff in rehearsal for *The Tempest* (2010).

harsh words or judgments," he says, "and here is Shakespeare in *Cymbeline*, getting to do exactly that. You go back, through dreams. At the end of your life, in your seventies or eighties, you look back and wish that certain elements of your life were different, and none of us has the ability to do that. It's why the classics are so important, because we don't live long enough to ever be able to set the world right. By the time we learn everything, we're dead.

"Shakespeare wrote this play when he was my age. We get the sense of a man who is recreating his life through his art—something we never get to do in life. And there's this incredibly happy ending. The king returns to his kingdom, he gets back the two sons he'd lost; his relationship with his daughter, which was terrible, becomes positive; then his wife—whom he's never gotten along with—dies, so that's part of the happy ending too."

Cymbeline is a hybrid of sorts. Appearing in the First Folio of Shakespeare's works under the title *The Tragedie of Cymbeline*, it is often staged as comedy, while scholars since the nineteenth century have classed it as a romance. British novelist Anthony Burgess called it "the most curious of all Shakespeare's mixtures." This ambivalence is one reason why it is so rarely performed—and lack of performance, of course, means that the play remains largely unfamiliar to audiences.

"If you're doing something like *Cymbeline*," Cimolino says, "you have to keep in mind that most people won't have seen it. So you need to have narrative clarity. It isn't the same as, say, *A Midsummer Night's Dream*, which most people will have seen already, perhaps in several versions. With that degree of familiarity to rely on, you can sometimes experiment a bit more. That said, I didn't opt for a traditional staging of *Cymbeline*. As an artist, you still have to follow your instincts.

"I centred the production around dreams. I wanted to explore dreams as a way of healing. Posthumus—who is a commoner adopted by the royal household—has a dream that his parents come back. They ask the gods

On Directing the Solo Performer

It might seem that the easiest job a director could have is a one-person show: it is theatre reduced to its essence. There are no battle scenes, no complex staging of multiple characters, no big musical numbers. Yet the one-man (or one-woman) play can be one of the biggest challenges in theatre.

"I thought directing a one-man play might be a bit easier," says Des McAnuff, "but I found you couldn't turn away for even a second"

Before tackling Christopher Plummer's *A Word or Two* in 2012, the only solo show Des McAnuff had directed was Billy Crystal's *700 Sundays*, a popular and critical hit during its 2005 Broadway run. "I thought directing a one-man play might be a bit easier," McAnuff says of that experience, "but I found you couldn't turn away for even a second. With a big production, you might have the fight director take over for a bit, or the choreographer. But you can't with a one-man show. It really is unbelievably exhausting."

One of the keys to the one-man show is the one man, of course. In Christopher Plummer, McAnuff has one of the best actors in the world—one whose earlier solo play, *Barrymore* (technically a two-hander, though only Plummer's character is seen on stage), won him a Tony Award on Broadway. It was revived in Toronto in 2011 with great success. "With Mr. Plummer, you have a great artist," McAnuff says. "And he is someone you want to spend two hours with."

Christopher Plummer at a gala in his honour held in Toronto on September 26, 2011, at which he received the Festival's inaugural Lifetime Achievement Award.

to protect him. And he wakes up from that dream a different man. The play is an exploration of our ability to heal when reality is no comfort. So we look to dreams."

In Shakespeare's work, dreams play a significant role. In *Richard III*, Richard wakes from a dream asking: "Is there a murderer here? No. Yes, I am." It is in dreams sometimes, that the truth is found. We see it in Lady Macbeth's nightmares, or Hamlet's fear that death might not end dreaming: "For in that sleep of death what dreams may come." As Prospero says in *The Tempest*, "We are such stuff / As dreams are made on."

The analysis of the text, which Cimolino does first on his own, then in concert with scholars and a dramaturge, includes examining the characters. The character Iachimo is Italian. "At the time," Cimolino says, "the English impression of Italians was largely based on Machiavelli: they were thought to be sinister and clever. But Iachimo is the first man in the play to see how beautiful Innogen actually is. I have perhaps a different sense of this character. I cast Tom McCamus as Iachimo—women are all in love with Tom. But the point is, you go through that process with each character. And your impressions of the character may be radically different than what has been done by others. And that is gold."

The director brings his own views, but ultimately they must serve the text. Tyrone Guthrie once wrote: "That your own interpretation of a work of art is flagrantly subjective seems to be regarded as an arrogant attitude. But the truer view is that the interpretive artist can only make his own comment upon the work." Guthrie's view on what the director does remains one of the most encompassing: "The director is partly an artist presiding over a group of other artists, excitable, unruly, childlike and intermittently 'inspired.' He is also the foreman of a factory, the abbot of a monastery, and the superintendent of an analytic laboratory. It will do no harm if, in addition to other weapons, he arms himself with the patience of a good nurse, together with the voice and vocabulary of an old-time sergeant-major."

Facing page: Director Ethan McSweeny with company members Jennifer Stewart, Naomi Costain (Edith) and assistant director Darcy Evans in rehearsal for *The Pirates of Penzance* (2012). Above: Director Antoni Cimolino and Tom McCamus (Iachimo) in rehearsal for *Cymbeline* (2012).

Chapter Four

Truth Under Imaginary Circumstances: The Acting Company

The first lines to be uttered on a Stratford stage were spoken by Sir Alec Guinness playing Richard III in 1953: "Now is the winter of our discontent / Made glorious summer by this son of York." Guinness was unfazed by the sound of a train whistle as he performed on the stage beneath the tent. He was, however, slightly fazed by Ontario's curiously antiquated liquor laws, which at the time required customers to fill out a form that stated their names, addresses and what they intended to buy. "We were rather surprised," Guinness wrote in his autobiography, "that in Ontario we had to register at the local liquor store as alcoholics."

One of the oddest moments for an actor on a Stratford stage came when William Hutt was playing King Lear in 1972. The audience was filled with high school students on the day of the final game of the epic Canada-Russia hockey series. During the matinée, Paul Henderson scored his mythic goal, sealing the outcome. The audience knew the game was likely over, but didn't know who had won. A radio backstage kept the actors and crew informed, though. As he exited a scene, Hutt turned to the audience and uttered the welcome, un-Shakespearean words, "Henderson scores. Canada wins." The applause was deafening.

Theatre starts with the word, but actors are the most visible face of the Festival. Over the years many great actors have been part of it: William Hutt, Douglas Campbell, Christopher Plummer, Frances Hyland,

Martha Henry, Maggie Smith, Seana McKenna, Stephen Ouimette, Lucy Peacock, Brian Bedford, Colm Feore. There are actors who started at Stratford and became famous elsewhere: Lorne Greene (who played Brutus in *Julius Caesar* before he went on to become Pa Cartwright); William Shatner (who played Lucius in *Julius Caesar* and understudied Christopher Plummer as Henry V before Captain Kirk). Other stars who have come to Stratford include Paul Scofield, Peter Ustinov, Alan Bates, Jessica Tandy, Hume Cronyn, Christopher Walken (who, some may be surprised to learn, played Romeo in 1968) and Brian Dennehy.

Des McAnuff has called it the best repertory company in the world. "We are a Shakespearean theatre," he says, "so at centre stage you are going to find the plays of William Shakespeare. But we also have all kinds of talents and skills and muscles that affect other areas. One of the things that made me very proud of *Jesus Christ Superstar* is the fact that I had my Orlando [Paul Nolan, who played that role in *As You Like It*] as Jesus, I had my Jaques [Brent Carver, also from *As You Like It*] as Pilate, I had our Rose of Sharon [Chilina Kennedy, from *The Grapes of Wrath*] as Mary Magdalene. These people can do contemporary twentieth-century plays and Shakespeare, and they can also sing one of the most ambitious rock-and-roll scores of recent times. That's a remarkable group of artists to work with and lead."

The Festival employs 110 to 130 actors each year for nine months, which is unique in North America. "We've been able to build an extraordinary company of actors," says Antoni Cimolino, "who don't need to make a living doing ketchup commercials, as is maybe the case in the United States. It's hard to make a living in theatre in the U.S., impossible to make your living doing classical theatre. In Canada, we have this great group of actors who are great classical actors first and foremost. So Denzel Washington doesn't come, but that's okay. Over time, we create our own stars."

Stratford's acting company is one of the most crucial aspects of the Festival's success. Acting has been defined as "acting truthfully under imaginary

Company members in the curtain call for *Camelot*.

Hitting the Road

In February and March each year, Associate Artistic Director Dean Gabourie and Casting Director Beth Russell spend a month auditioning actors in major cities across Canada. Their mission: to meet with actors who have not had an opportunity to audition for the Festival before and to increase the diversity of the company with performers who can handle the classical repertoire. "We're looking for clarity of thought, precision of speech, connection to the emotions and an ease with verse and text," says Gabourie.

For approximately eight hours a day, they audition at least six people an hour, breaking only for lunch. In the evenings, they generally take in a play. "It helps us keep our fingers on the pulse of what's going on in the nation," says Gabourie. "What you discover, doing this from coast to coast, is that there are *flavours*, from Vancouver to St. John's: different regional strengths both in individual actors and in their theatre communities.

"It's also important for us to be ambassadors for the Festival, to make sure everyone understands that Stratford is interested in and accessible to actors from all across the country."

Associate Artistic Director Dean Gabourie.

circumstances" and, more obliquely, as "standing up naked and turning around slowly." It has been stated simply as "listening" or "creating relationships" or "emotional discovery." Sara Topham (Olivia in *Twelfth Night*) says: "The actor goes through dozens of permutations, in rehearsal, with the director, with voice coaches, with costume and wigmakers, making discoveries and choices, but the result on stage should feel inevitable. At its best, acting is invisible."

The first step is matching actors to parts. Wherever possible, artists already in the company will be given first consideration. "Our first responsibility is to the company," says Casting Director Beth Russell, who is in her fourth season at Stratford. "And if there isn't something for a particular artist next season, we will still keep them uppermost in our minds for the season after that."

Casting the principals essentially provides the skeleton, and the rest of the roles are added afterward, fleshing out the cast. In February, eighteen months before a season begins, Russell travels the country with Associate Artistic Director Dean Gabourie, holding general auditions and staying in touch with the various acting communities. Then, once the season has been announced (usually in June for a season that opens a year later), Russell schedules auditions for specific roles in that upcoming season with each of the directors assigned to the plays.

"The biggest challenge at Stratford," she says, "is the cross-casting. As we are a repertory company, actors are required to be cast in two or three plays and must be adept with not only classical but also contemporary text. And some actors cross into the musicals as well, which requires singing and dancing skills. That makes the casting process longer and more involved."

Additionally, there is the challenge of working within the master schedule, which outlines rehearsal hours and performance days and times for each production.

Chilina Kennedy (Lois Lane / Bianca) and Julius Sermonia (Dance Captain / Nathaniel) with company members in rehearsal for *Kiss Me, Kate* (2010).

Top: Company members in rehearsal for *Jesus Christ Superstar* (2011). Above: company members in rehearsal for *Kiss Me, Kate* (2010). Facing page: Company members in rehearsal for *42nd Street* (2012).

Left: Designer Santo Loquasto, wardrobe lead hand Laurie Krempien-Hall (left) and cutter Margaret Lamb with Seana McKenna (la Marquise de Merteuil) in a costume fitting for *Dangerous Liaisons* (2010). Right: Chilina Kennedy (Eva Perón) with Margaret Lamb in a costume fitting for *Evita* (2010).

An actor might be ideally suited for roles in two different productions—but if those productions "play against" each other (meaning that performances of them are scheduled for the same dates and times), then obviously the actor cannot be in both. It may also be that more than one director wants the same actor. Casting is a multi-layered process that involves the actor, multiple directors and sometimes a musical director and a choreographer as well as the Artistic Director and Casting Director.

The actors begin to arrive as early as January for costume and wig fittings. Depending on when the play opens, rehearsals can start in February. They go from 10 a.m. to 6 p.m. six days a week for up to eight weeks. One of the luxuries of Stratford is the amount of rehearsal time the actors have. In regional theatre it can be as little as two weeks. Two weeks isn't enough time to settle into a leading Shakespeare role and to inhabit the character, find the rhythms of the text. One Stratford actor says, "It's in week three that I usually go: 'I don't know how to act, I don't know how I'm going to get away with this and they should just fire me now.'" A long rehearsal period helps overcome the natural insecurities of the actor.

One of the central challenges of repertory theatre is playing two or three roles each season, so rehearsals alternate between different projects and between disparate characters, each presenting unique challenges. In 2008, Ben Carlson first came to Stratford to play Hamlet, one of the most demanding roles in theatre. That season he also played Tranio in *The Taming of the Shrew* and Dumaine in *All's Well That Ends Well*.

"Doing three roles in three different plays," says Carlson, "is imaginatively exhausting because you have to create three different worlds and you have to sustain them over a long run." This is heightened by the fact that at Stratford, an actor could be going from Shakespeare's language in the matinée to a contemporary British accent in the evening, or going between tragedy and comedy.

Ben Carlson (Touchstone) with cutter Terri Dans in a costume fitting for *As You Like It* (2010).

Top: Tom Rooney (Master Ford) and Lucy Peacock (Mistress Ford) in rehearsal for *The Merry Wives of Windsor* (2011). Above left: Nora McLellan (Flora Van Huysen) in rehearsal for *The Matchmaker* (2012). Above right: Geraint Wyn Davies (Cymbeline), Yanna McIntosh (Queen) and Cara Ricketts (Innogen) with members of the company in rehearsal for *Cymbeline* (2012). Facing page: Company members in rehearsal for *The Pirates of Penzance* (2012).

In 2011 Carlson played Feste, the fool in *Twelfth Night*. "The last two years I've been playing fools—last year as Feste, the year before as Touchstone in *As You Like It*—and that was a lot of fun. Which is surprising, because years ago someone asked me what scared me most about Shakespeare, and I said, 'The fools.' Because they're supposed to be funny. And it's hard for that comedy to reach a modern audience. A lot of the jokes are antiquated and elusive. I thought it was the hardest thing. Well, Hamlet was the hardest thing. But after that. . . . Comedy's hard."

Lucy Peacock, who has spent twenty-five seasons at Stratford, says doing multiple roles for a sustained run is a bit like the Olympics. "A two-show day is a twelve-hour day, at least," she says. "By October, it becomes about stamina, along with all the other challenges." Her stamina was tested in 2006 when she played Beatrice in *Much Ado About Nothing*, the title character in *The Duchess of Malfi* and seven different characters (including a man) in the one-woman play *The Blonde, the Brunette and the Vengeful Redhead*. Often she had two of these shows a day.

How to keep all those people compartmentalized over the course of several months? "My characters had to behave themselves," she says. "They had to be kept in check until it was time to get going. With nine people jockeying for position inside my head and my body, I really had to be strict with myself—or maybe it's more a case of being strict with them. They weren't allowed to stretch their muscles until it was their turn. You boot up for one show, then you turn off the computer, and you reboot for the next show. But inevitably you take the experience of the matinée into the evening performance. It will always be a unique result. That day, those shows, in that way, will never be repeated."

Left: Lucy Peacock (Morgan le Fay) prepares for a performance of *Camelot*. Facing page: Brian Dennehy (Sir Toby Belch), Ben Carlson (Feste) and Stephen Ouimette (Sir Andrew Aguecheek) with members of the company in rehearsal for *Twelfth Night*.

Bruce Dow prepares for his role as King Herod in *Jesus Christ Superstar* (2011).

Some playwrights are more strenuous than others. "Chekhov is the spa," she says. "Shakespeare is extreme sports. I've always felt there was a natural endorphin that kicks in for actors that's like women in childbirth. You go through that agony and think, 'Why would I ever think of doing this again?' But you do, because it is a labour of love, pure and simple."

Doing more than one role can be especially taxing if they involve singing and/or dancing. Bruce Dow, who has had twelve seasons at Stratford and in 2011 played a scene-stealing King Herod in *Jesus Christ Superstar* as well as Squire Dap in *Camelot*, says, "You're singing *Camelot* in the afternoon, which is a classic Broadway score with a very particular sound, and then in the evening you're singing *Jesus Christ Superstar*, which is contemporary rock with a particular sound—that's very taxing on the voice.

"The dance too: there's hip hop and acrobatics with *Superstar*, then more traditional movement in *Camelot*. At non-repertory theatres, you perform a standard eight-show-a-week schedule—a repeated series of evening and matinée performances of the same show—so your body finds a rhythm. With Stratford, you've got the challenge of two productions, but they never come at the same time in the week and they change from afternoon to evening, so your body is always in shock. It's more evident with people my age, where the body can't bounce back as easily, but also in the youngest artists who haven't done it before. It's horrific."

And there is the challenge of working with different directors and their approaches to the work. Some are actors' directors, others are more focused on the text. Some start the process with a speech, or a design presentation, or a read-through. They have different emphases, different temperaments.

For Des McAnuff, perhaps because he is a writer as well, the text is supreme. With *Jesus Christ Superstar*, the cast spent the first three days discussing the musical with the dramaturge: the history, origins and themes, the writers, and previous productions.

"It begins with a process I call 'sleuthing,' " McAnuff says, "poring over the text with dictionaries and reference books at hand, making sure that every word, and every nuance of every word, is properly understood. As an actor, you have to intimately understand not only your own lines but the entire text. The next part of the process is to personalize the text, to bring emotion to it, to pour your own soul into the language. And then finally, when you are so comfortable with the text that you can make it experiential, when there is no separation between the thought, the word and the emotion, you go on a journey of discovery and revelation."

"Voice connects us to the essence of what it is to be human"

For this journey, McAnuff usually employs a dramaturge. "For *Jesus Christ Superstar*, I used Chad Silvain," he says. "It was like graduate school: we studied the bible, the Gospels, looked at the historical context and talked about other productions as well. We read Tim Rice's autobiography. There were twenty-eight people around the table. We went through page by page, attaching notes to the libretto." They examined the Last Supper and what it meant in Judaism and Christianity.

It can take three days to go through the dramaturgical process. "Des expects you to absorb and understand that, and that it will inform your work," says Dow. "He's like a strict teacher. You come away with something you can work with. He trusts you to do that work."

Herod's song—"So you are the Christ, you're the great Jesus Christ, prove to me that you're no fool, walk across my swimming pool"—is usually treated as a cabaret number. "It's the 11 o'clock number," Dow says. "Structurally, it's the number that gives the audience relief before the dénouement. But Des wanted it to tell the story too. So it had a definite dramatic purpose in our production.

"Des expects you to do so much on your own. He's an incredibly trusting man; he'll let you go. He'll get into a scene and say, 'This has to happen,' but it's up to you to make it happen. In *Superstar*, the one direction I remember is, 'Don't touch Jesus.' That was it. '*Don't touch Jesus.*' "

Stella Adler, the famous acting coach, said that when you stand on a stage, "you must have a sense that you are addressing the whole world, and that what you say is so important the whole world must listen." Actors may appear to have a natural physical and vocal presence, but in fact they commit many hours to the ongoing development of their bodies and voices as expressive instruments. The Festival employs a team of twelve voice, text, movement and Alexander technique coaches who work to support the actors in meeting the demands of the theatre spaces and the plays. In a season, the coaching team give more than three thousand sessions to actors, both before and during a play's run. Actors are required to vocally fill the space and move with ease and sensitivity. Their bodies and voices need to convey character, emotion and nuance. They also need to survive a long, often arduous season.

At a deeper level, voice is the embodiment of the artist. "I would say that anyone who is coaching or teaching voice," says Janine Pearson, Head of Voice and Coaching at Stratford, "somewhere along the line has been looking for their own voice and struggling to find that voice at the most profound level. What is voice? It's not just standing up on a stage and sounding beautiful. It connects us to the essence of what it is to be human, of what it is to have a voice in the world. You must have a really strong understanding of the voice: physically, emotionally, psychically, spiritually and, finally, psychosomatically."

With actors, as with Olympic athletes, the expertise of a professional coach helps make an already superb skill-set better. The process of coaching includes working with accents and dialects, mining the text and making certain that the actor has a physical and vocal instrument open and available to both the play

and the director's vision. For many artists, the voice and movement work can be a way into the character, so this work begins in the rehearsal process. Once a production is open, however, most of the work evolves around supporting the demands on the actor, which can become more pronounced as the run goes on.

The different roles that actors play in repertory rarely have anything in common. To move between the Dust Bowl Oklahomans in *The Grapes of Wrath* and the ancient Romans of *Titus Andronicus*—or the aesthetes in Molière's *The Misanthrope*—requires vastly different ways of talking and moving.

"Both men and women wear high heels in Molière, and wigs, and the crispness of their diction is reflective of their wit, status and manners," says Pearson. "Then all of a sudden you're these Oklahomans who are connected to the earth, who have spent much of their summers in bare feet, their hands in the ground, who have so much dust blowing around they close off their noses—and that's why their voices get a bit nasal. That sound, the way they use their bodies, that connection to what's happening to them, that defeat that's happening in their bodies, all of that goes into the transformation of the body and voice for that play."

Both Brian Dennehy and Stephen Ouimette had to switch between the east London accents of *The Homecoming* and the Elizabethan language of *Twelfth Night*, often on a daily basis (though the relationship between their respective characters in those plays was oddly similar). Finding the nuances and rhythm of those accents takes time. Sometimes the dialectical differences can be subtle. In *The Homecoming*, Mike Shara was playing Teddy, the brother who had gone to live in America, so his accent was slightly different from those of his siblings and his father.

Brian Dennehy first came to Stratford in 2008 after working with Festival alumnus Christopher Plummer on Broadway. "Three roles," Dennehy says: "Beckett [*Krapp's Last Tape*], O'Neill [*Hughie*] and Shakespeare [the King of France in *All's Well That Ends Well*]. After two weeks, you're thinking, 'What have I done?' But

Facing page: Participants in the Festival's 2012 Birmingham Conservatory for Classical Theatre in a coaching session. Above: Actor Lucy Peacock (left) works with Head of Voice and Coaching Janine Pearson.

Head of Voice and Coaching Janine Pearson works with participants in the 2012 Birmingham Conservatory.

Stratford is a very special place if you're a serious actor. It's like Camelot for an actor."

If an actor is doing two or three roles, especially if singing is involved, coaches help with the maintenance of the voice over the season by peeling away physical tensions or habits that might inhibit the freedom of their sound. Actors protect themselves in various ways, often committing to lengthy pre-performance warm-ups in addition to daily physical and vocal conditioning routines and limiting their participation in social events so that they can rest within the gruelling demands of their work. To save themselves for the moments when they are on stage, they often have to sacrifice a personal life that most of us would take for granted.

The theatre spaces at Stratford are very different and make different demands on the actors and on their voices. The Festival Theatre, with over eighteen hundred seats, is the largest space, yet it's surprisingly intimate; the most distant seat is only sixty-six feet from the stage. The proscenium-arch Avon is smaller, yet it is 119 feet to the back row. At the Tom Patterson Theatre, with its elongated thrust, distances vary considerably. The Studio Theatre is small but the audience seating has a steep rake. Each has its own aural signature and requires the actor to adjust his voice and delivery accordingly.

The physical spaces affect how the part is played. With the thrust stage, the actor is effectively in the audience, and actors respond to that vulnerability in various ways. The standard line with thrust stages is that the actor is exposed: there's no place to hide. Although as Ben Carlson (Benedick in 2012's *Much Ado About Nothing* and Fluellen in *Henry V*) notes, "You're an actor. You're not *supposed* to be hiding on the stage. I love the thrust stage, and not just for Shakespeare. But especially for him, because there are so many monologues that are given directly to the audience. And you're not pretending you're alone. You're actually talking to an audience." The thrust stage also means that most of the time, the actor will have his back to at least some part of the audience, another acoustic hurdle.

"It requires a lot of voice to fill the Festival Theatre," Carlson says. "For film and TV, when there's a microphone on your collar, you don't need *any* voice. You can actually do a part with *no* vocal projection. But in the Stratford theatres, you need to project, you need training, and you need to keep working on your voice."

With the thrust stage, the actor is among the audience rather than before it, an acquired taste for many actors.

"When I first worked on it," Mike Shara says, "I felt like a fish on a bicycle, but later on I found it liberating." Lucy Peacock says the thrust stage is like Shakespeare: it can set you free, but it can also reveal your limitations.

It does add another level of vulnerability to what is already a vulnerable profession. "An actor is totally vulnerable," Alec Guinness once said. "His total personality is exposed to critical judgment—his intellect, his bearing, his diction, his whole appearance. In short, his ego."

Voice coaches help with singing roles and adapting to a microphone. Most musical-theatre productions at Stratford use microphones concealed in the performers' wigs, though *Jesus Christ Superstar* used what is now referred to as the Madonna mike: a microphone that, while still discreet, is worn near the actor's mouth. "Using a mike is a technical skill that is as different as thrust versus proscenium," says Bruce Dow. "I love working on mike because you can do so many different things with your voice. Most musicals written after 1970 are written for an amplified voice. If you listen to an old Rodgers and Hammerstein score, there is a light orchestration under the voice, and the music happens between phrases. Since the 1970s, in musicals—and not just rock—the orchestration has become more complex and you need a microphone to be heard. Microphones aren't cheating. It helps you get the musicality in the score. But it is a different skill."

Voice and text coaches also work with the actor to discover the muscularity and sense of language. At the beginning of rehearsals, they work with actors on meaning, emphasis, punctuation and the rhythm of the lines, especially with Shakespeare. Janine Pearson starts by reading the play out loud several times, then does the lexical research, looking up unfamiliar words or colloquialisms. She compares Shakespeare's Folio edition with modern editions such as Penguin or Oxford. "The coach hopes to assist the actor in unlocking the meaning of a line," she says.

Sometimes the role calls for not just an accent or dialect but another language. "My first two speaking parts here were in foreign languages," says Sara

Guest instructor Valerie Moore works with participants in the 2012 Conservatory.

Paul Nolan (Vicomte de Valvert) and Colm Feore (Cyrano) rehearse a fight scene for *Cyrano de Bergerac* (2009).

Topham, who has been at Stratford for twelve years. "First in French, which I have only a high school command of, and then in *Henry IV*, I played Lady Mortimer, and I had to speak in Welsh—which I had never spoken. I worked *very* closely with the voice coach.

"The voice coaches are an amazing resource here, and I work with them regardless of what the requirements of the play are. If I don't have an accent I still work with a coach, because they do . . . *everything*. These plays require a great deal from you. The coaches can help you with your breath, with connecting to the human aspect, to working out a scene. Sometimes you go to a voice coach and all you'll do is have a conversation. Often you know there's a problem, something doesn't feel right, and a voice coach can

help you identify it. Sometimes you have to work around the scene to see why you are having trouble telling the story. We're trying to create living human beings on the stage, and we use pieces of ourselves and pieces of the character, and you try and bring those things together so the audience doesn't see any separation between you and the character. For me, the coaches are a hugely important part of that process."

Lucy Peacock says, "The sophistication of the voice work that is done here is not just about stamina or health, though late in the season it can be about that. A lot of the initial work is done in rehearsal but it evolves as you transform yourself alongside the realization of the character, both technically and emotionally."

Voice is key to so many characters, but to Richard III it is absolutely critical. His voice needs to be seductive—

how else to seduce the wife of a man you've murdered? His conversation is insistent throughout the play. It is through the power of speech that Richard essentially imposes his reality on the world. When Seana McKenna played Richard in 2011 (becoming the first female actor to do so at Stratford), her voice was by turns intimate and piercing. It both masked and personified his evil, a tricky balance.

Even more than voice though, Richard is associated with movement. The way he moves is a benchmark of Shakespearean theatre. Will he limp? How hunched will he be? And how does he carry that withered arm? When McKenna played Richard, one arm was built up so that her normal feminine arm appeared withered in comparison. Movement coaches work to establish a gait and a stance that facilitate what the actor wants to communicate and that are practical for the gruelling run.

Movement on stage ranges from the subtle (how does Willy Loman's posture signal his defeat?) to the raucous (the swordfights in *Titus Andronicus*). For the former there are movement coaches, for the latter, a fight coach. "In *Titus Andronicus*," says fight director Simon Fon, "every ninety-seven lines somebody has an act of violence done to them. It averages 5.2 atrocities per act."

Fon learned his craft while taking a fine arts degree at York University, where he also did a bit of fencing. He studied martial arts, in which he has a black belt, and has been trained in various weapons. For any production, Fon starts with historical research: would a Roman legionnaire fight differently from a centurion? How would they wear their sword belts, how would they draw their swords? "What is that first moment of physical violence and interaction going to be?" Fon asks.

In the case of *Titus Andronicus*, Fon then talked to director Darko Tresnjak to see how he wanted to approach the violence. They went through the play over the phone then again in person, mapping a strategy. It was modified once the actors arrived and they were dealing with the spatial limitations of the stage. "As we're building an act of violence," Fon says, "it's important that the actors get a sense of breathing and balance. We begin very slowly. It's a dance—a dance of death, but nonetheless a dance."

The weapons are made of aluminum (or sometimes rubber) and are blunted, but they can be dangerous nonetheless. It takes about twenty hours to choreograph and rehearse a two-minute stage fight. "It's important," Fon says, "for actors to be able to live within a fight scene." Even if, as is the case in *Titus*, they are going to end up dying.

"Sometimes I dream of revolution," says Moon in Tom Stoppard's *The Real Inspector Hound*: "troupes of actors slaughtered by their understudies." The understudy's job is an odd one that contains both the hope of playing a cherished role and the fear of actually having to play it.

It is one of the most difficult jobs in acting. There is the need to have the part perfectly memorized, with the

Claire Lautier (Tamora) and Sean Arbuckle (Saturninus) rehearse a scene in *Titus Andronicus* (2011) with director Darko Tresnjak (centre). Watching in the background are Amanda Lisman (Lavinia) and Skye Brandon (Bassianus).

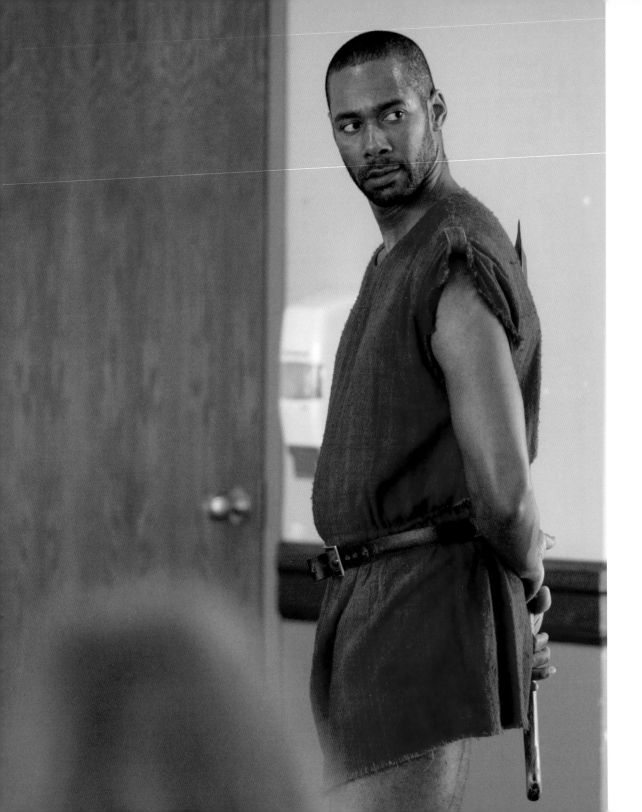

knowledge that you may never go on. You're required to sign a contract agreeing to be ready if necessary, yet you don't get much rehearsal time. Understudies do have their own rehearsal, but usually not until the play has already begun its run; and then they have only two five-hour blocks on the actual stage (one for rehearsal and one for a run of the play) which have to accommodate all the understudies—many of whom may be understudying more than one role.

"There are three things you can do if you're an understudy," says stage manager Ann Stuart. "You can watch rehearsals with your principal [the actor being understudied], and then you hear what the director is saying. Or you can talk to the principal, though not every principal wants this. Or the assistant directors may work with the understudies." Understudies also make healthy use of the coaches' time, adds Janine Pearson.

To complicate matters, the understudy is usually already playing another part in the play. "I did a lot of understudy work for a long time and never went on," says Sara Topham, recalling her earlier years at the Festival. "Then I was playing Jessica and understudying Portia in *The Merchant of Venice*. I was waiting at the intermission and the stage manager came over and said to me, 'Um, Severn [Thompson] is sick, so she's going home.' And I was thinking, 'Why is he telling me this?' I actually didn't make the connection. And he looked at me and said, 'So you're playing Portia.'

"I had five minutes to get into her costume and her wig, which were still warm. I put them on and the stage manager said, 'Do you need anything?' I needed the costume and wig people to talk me through the quick changes, because there were five quick changes that I'd never done. Because as an understudy, you never wear the costume, ever. So they talked me through the quick changes and I stood backstage waiting to make my entrance—I had the first line of the second act. And as the lights went down, I said to the people backstage, 'Does anyone know my first line?'

"They laughed. They thought I was joking. But in that moment, your mind is completely blank. I walked out on

Facing page: Dion Johnstone (Aaron) in a rehearsal for *Titus Andronicus* (2011). Above: Fight director Simon Fon works on a fight scene for *Peter Pan* (2010).

Above: Cara Ricketts (Maria) gets help with her wig in preparation for a performance of *Twelfth Night*. Facing page: A backstage view of the curtain call for *The Grapes of Wrath* (2011).

stage not knowing in my head what the first line was. But my *body* knew my first line. And once that was out, it was great, then my head kicked in and did what it was supposed to do. Your body remembers somehow. It's a bit like you've watched the surgery channel a whole lot and suddenly you have a scalpel in your hand and a live body in front of you. It was the most exhilarating and horrifying experience."

In a performance of *Camelot* last year, five people were out, including Geraint Wyn Davies in the lead role of King Arthur. His understudy was Stratford veteran Sandy Winsby, who was playing Sir Sagramore. This made for a somewhat Freudian situation on stage, since Lancelot was being played by his son, Jonathan Winsby. Jonathan, in turn, went on for Paul Nolan as Jesus in *Jesus Christ Superstar*, and did a brilliant job.

When an understudy comes on, it can change the texture of the play. His performance may be more comic, or less so; her singing may be textured differently. An understudy may not hit the marks with the same accuracy as the principal, and the nuances are different, the rhythms subtly altered. So the cast rallies around them. The audience sometimes rallies around them too. Occasionally the change is so seamless the audience fails to notice.

The audience, it has been said, is fifty percent of the performance. It is surprising how different they can be from show to show. Sometimes the audience changes between acts: quiet during the first act of a comedy, raucous in the second. The audience enters the theatre as an assembly of individuals, but by the final curtain they can become a single entity, whether responsive, mute, angry or restless. They are an evolving, complex, bloody-minded organism. Orson Welles said you can't give the audience too much or they won't work with you. "That's what gives the theatre meaning," he said. "When it becomes a social act."

In this electronic age, where interaction with screens often supersedes interaction with people, theatre remains one of the most social acts. Without the audience, the show doesn't exist. In Shakespeare's

The audience, it has been said, is fifty percent of the performance

plays, the audience often has a role. "They're like the last character," says Sara Topham, "particularly in a play like *Twelfth Night*. They are the only ones who know Viola's secrets; they're Viola's acting partner. They have more information than Olivia does and that impacts Olivia."

Christopher Plummer, whose Stratford pedigree goes back to 1956, would agree. "The public is your partner," he once said in a newspaper interview. "A lot of people think you have to play straight to your leading lady and never take in the fact there's an audience. How wrong! It's so exciting to bounce off an audience—if things are going well. If things are going badly, they are the first to tell you. But there's nothing like a live audience."

The audience demographic at Stratford has a particularly wide range, from busloads of students to busloads of seniors to everyone in between. It can make for a curious dynamic and a wildly varied experience.

"With a more mature audience, you have certain guarantees," says Ben Carlson. "They've been conditioned to respond in a theatre. With student audiences there are more variables. They'll let you know exactly what they think. It's challenging, and in a way it's the most important audience you could ever have, because they will grow up and either go or not go to the theatre, and part of that responsibility lies with us."

"I'm one of the people who loves student audiences," says Bruce Dow. "Because they'll tell you right away if you're lying or being pretentious. I've been in a couple of productions here where there has been a polite response from an older audience; then the students come in. If you have a show that is really working, they are with you all the way, and they'll tell you before everyone else. Students are more vocal. When they are into the play, they will murmur about what's going on—in a good way. If they are detached, talking, bored and shifting in their seats, more often than not it's because we haven't done our job. We're not telling the story. We're being self-indulgent. The fault lies not with the

students but with the production and the actors."

He once attempted to rebuke a particularly obnoxious student. "I turned and stared at this girl, a look that said, 'How dare you? We are great artists.' She gave me the finger. And I thought, 'You're so right.' It can be very easy for an actor playing Shakespeare to get lost in the musicality or poetry of the piece. It's also easy to get lost in the intellectual or emotional acrobatics of the piece. And, if we are being totally honest, our egos can get in the way. It's very easy to go on stage and basically say no more to an audience than 'I am playing a Great Role in Shakespeare!' But a student audience will see right through all of that. They will call you out, and rightly so."

Geraint Wyn Davies, whose 2012 roles include Malachi Stack in *The Matchmaker* and the title role in *Cymbeline*, once took a more direct approach to an unruly audience member. "I was doing Hamlet in England," he says, "and there was a fellow in the audience who was so disruptive that when I got to the 'O what a rogue and peasant slave am I' speech, I went and sat on his lap, and did it all while sitting there. It was a bold and crazy move. I played it to him. He came up afterwards and thanked me. If you include them, hopefully they join in."

Wyn Davies recalls how unruly student audiences used to be at Stratford twenty-five years ago. When she was a stage manager, Nora Polley used to keep all the things the kids threw on the stage: jelly beans, pennies, pieces of asphalt. Her collection, encased in a Lucite box, now sits in the Archives and looks like the contents of a shark's stomach.

"Stratford's mandate is to do the great works of the theatre," Ben Carlson says. "That's a great mandate. It's a large mountain to have to climb all the time, but that's the reason I've always wanted to work here." And what are the rewards of being an actor? Washington Irving said an actor's fulfillment was in being unfulfilled. Like life, you could always have done it better.

Facing page: Without the audience, the show doesn't exist—a dance number from *West Side Story* (2009).
Right: A view of *Camelot* from the stage left vomitorium.

An Immersion Course in Classical Theatre

In 1998, Richard Monette, who was then the Festival's Artistic Director, started what is now the Birmingham Conservatory for Classical Theatre, designed to help train actors for classical repertoires. It was run first by Michael Mawson, then by David Latham and now (since 2007) by celebrated actor and director Martha Henry.

"The Conservatory began," says Henry, "because Richard found that in auditioning young actors they didn't have any text skills. They couldn't speak, didn't know how to pronounce words, how to construct a sentence. They stressed illogical words in the audition and didn't know how to handle the text, often didn't know what it meant. Despite the quality of the actors, any classical skills seemed to have gone down the drain, so to speak."

The program started as a three-week intensive course at the end of the season. Monette selected actors who he thought had promise but weren't yet comfortable with Shakespeare, and they were trained in movement and text, starting at 8 a.m. and sometimes going until 10 p.m. The following year the program was extended to seven weeks. Finally it was shifted to the winter months and now runs for twenty weeks. Each year's graduates join the acting ensemble for the upcoming season.

An intensive search for candidates is conducted every two years by Henry and Casting Director Beth Russell. "We start in Newfoundland," says Henry, "and go across the country to Vancouver, and we also go to Chicago because

Left: Company member Stephen Ouimette (centre) works with Conservatory participants Alden Adair (left) and Brad Hodder.

"The sheer 'gasp effect' of walking out onto that stage"

there is an organization there called the Chicago Associates, who sponsor a young Chicago actor every year. We have about five hundred applicants and we see two hundred and fifty actors. From that we pick between thirteen and seventeen people and bring them to Stratford, and Des [McAnuff] auditions them. Out of that group we pick between six and ten."

Choreographers teach them everything from Elizabethan galliards to hip hop

The actors have a chance to work with Stratford's elite: such artists as Seana McKenna, Lucy Peacock, Ben Carlson. They see the shows, go backstage, work on text and skills, and are tutored in the delicate politics of a large theatre. (What do dressers really think of actors? What does a stage manager expect from them?) They get time on the thrust stage at the Festival Theatre

Facing page: Conservatory participants Bethany Jillard and Victor Dolhai. This page: The participants present their final rehearsal of *A Midsummer Night's Dream*.

to work with voice teachers on clarity, on volume and on what Henry calls "the sheer 'gasp effect' of walking out onto that stage."

Choreographers teach them everything from Elizabethan galliards to hip hop. Voice and movement coaches from Stratford and from other theatres or universities come in to give seminars. There is mask work, yoga and martial arts training. They take ballet. It is a rare opportunity for a crash course in all aspects of the stage, taught by some of the world's renowned teachers. "At the end of five months," says Henry, "they have had a pretty exceptional time."

They even learn how to handle criticism. "Because that is something you never get away from when you work in the theatre," Henry says. "You are constantly being critiqued, if not by a director or a teacher, then by a critic in print. You have someone writing about what they consider to be your failings. It's there for everyone to see, if not to remember."

Chapter Five

Setting the Scene

Desmond Heeley, one of the world's most acclaimed set and costume designers, has designed thirty-seven productions for Stratford, beginning in 1957. He is renowned among his colleagues for his ability to devise elaborate, sumptuous-looking sets using the most prosaic of materials: a magnificent "crystal" chandelier in 2009's *The Importance of Being Earnest*, for instance, was actually made out of plastic spoons and wine glasses. For one production, he specified no set at all: simply the unadorned bare stage that had been created by Tanya Moiseiwitsch for the Festival's first season in 1953. "And they *paid* you for this?" a colleague asked. Heeley's minimalist choice in that case wasn't an abdication of responsibility, however, but a return to the roots of Elizabethan theatre.

On the Elizabethan stage, they used minimal scenic effects. In the prologue to *Henry V*, the Chorus essentially asks the audience to conjure the battlefields of France. "Can this cockpit hold / The vasty fields of France? or may we cram / Within this wooden O the very casques / That did affright the air at Agincourt? . . . Piece out our imperfections with your thoughts." In other words, try and imagine the set.

The concept of creating the illusion of a place on stage arrived in England in the early seventeenth century, partway through Shakespeare's career. It was developed in Italy by Sebastiano Serlio, who explained the design of a court theatre in a book he published in 1545. At the time, Italian theatre spaces were usually

Right: Designer Desmond Heeley. Facing page: Heeley's design for Act I of *The Importance of Being Earnest* (2009).

in a large Hall of State. Perspective drawings, usually of cityscapes, acted as backdrop. The sets themselves were conceived in architectural terms; they weren't created to be moved.

It was British architect Inigo Jones who brought Italian Renaissance architecture to England, and along with it Serlio's ideas of set design. Jones introduced the concept of moveable scenery (as well as the proscenium arch) to London stages. He worked with Ben Jonson, Shakespeare's contemporary and occasional rival, and Jones and Jonson famously argued over which was more important in theatre, the sets or the text—an argument still heard on occasion.

In the nineteenth century there was a trend toward realism in sets, and in the 1850s Charles Kean's historically accurate productions of Shakespeare's histories dominated the London stage. This trend probably reached its apex in the twentieth century with American producer David Belasco, who built a working restaurant for one of his plays. Inevitably, there was a rebellion against realism, with designers looking for simpler, more evocative ways to express a sense of place. Nowadays, sets tend not to be naturalistic, but they are still regarded as making a vital contribution to the production's overall dramatic effect.

As the sets evolved, so did the role of set designer. "A designer," Buckminster Fuller said, "is an emerging synthesis of artist, mechanic, objective economist and evolutionary strategist." Nowhere is this more evident than in the theatre. Set designers must accommodate the play, the director's vision, their own aesthetic and the budget. Now, they must also accommodate technology, both in how their designs are conceived, and in the sets themselves, which increasingly involve automation.

Robert Brill, the New York-based designer of the 2012 season's production of *Henry V*, began his work at Stratford by laboriously creating in his computer a

Facing page: Assembling the floor for *Henry V* (2012). Right: Head of Automation Ian Phillips (left) and Technical Director Andrew Mestern in the scene shop.

Above Head of Properties Dona Hrabluk (left), designer Robert Brill and prop builder Heather Ruthig consult a taxidermy catalogue for parts to make a boar's head for *Henry V* (2012). Facing page, from left: Technical Director Andrew Mestern, scenic carpenter Simon Aldridge, designer Robert Brill and assistant set designer Devon Bhim measure the trap door in the Festival stage.

virtual model of the empty Festival Theatre. He and his team collated many years' worth of drawings and photographs of the theatre's interior, as seen from various angles, to build a surprisingly accurate three-dimensional rendering that allowed him to tailor his designs to the space. Using a program called 3D Studio MAX (favoured by the film industry for computer-generated special effects), he then generated three-dimensional virtual models of his sets, exporting these in turn to another program, Vectorworks, that enabled him to produce carpenter-friendly drawings.

Brill has worked with director Des McAnuff before, both at Stratford (*Caesar and Cleopatra*, *Macbeth*, *The Tempest*) and at La Jolla Playhouse (*The Wiz*, *Tartuffe*), so they have a professional understanding. In the summer of 2011 they met to discuss how they saw *Henry V* visually. Brill then created the castle, with its monochromatic wood tones, its height evoked by vertical beams, and its drawbridge providing some movement on stage.

Brill sent his designs to Andrew Mestern, Stratford's Technical Director, whose job it is to ensure that a designer's work gets properly translated into working drawings for the carpenters and to come up with a cost estimate. Mestern has a bearded counterculture look and an eclectic background that combines fine arts, welding, mechanics, draughtsmanship and AutoCAD, among other skills. After comparing the projected cost to the actual budget, some tweaking had to be done.

"For *Henry V*," Mestern says, "there's a large drawbridge that has to be very strong but very thin. We discussed the design requirements: How many people will be on it? How will we lift it?" Mestern talked to an engineer about the technical challenges. Then they had to figure out the best way to build it. "That's when I bring in Neil Cheney, the Head Carpenter."

An amiable man who grew up in Stratford, Cheney has worked at the Festival for thirty-eight years, as stagehand, scenic carpenter and now Head Carpenter. Standing in front of the almost-finished drawbridge, he describes the principal challenge that it posed: it

needed to be big (twenty feet by ten feet) and strong enough to bear the weight of all the actors who had to cross it, yet light enough to manoeuvre. "And the designer wanted light to come through the space between the planks. That made it more complex."

After trying various other approaches, Cheney settled on boards of quarter-inch plywood over a cardboard honeycomb core, framed by steel. The result, weighing about twelve hundred pounds, will be winched up on cables disguised to look like rope.

Printouts of Robert Brill's computer renderings are sitting nearby. They show detailed images of the wooden stage, the drawbridge and vertical beams. The verticals are going to be faux barn beams that come in twenty-foot lengths. Made of thin plywood, they aren't structural because Cheney needed something light and in one piece that would be easy to disassemble between shows. For structural beams, sometimes steel is dressed to look like wood. The result can be so convincing that it fools even the carpenters. On one occasion, a carpenter wanted to use part of an "oak beam"—actually a veneer glued over steel—that had been discarded from another set. Assuming it was solid oak, he tried to run his saw through it to cut it to the length he needed. When the blade hit the steel core, all its teeth were torn off.

The designers deliver their work in various forms. Debra Hanson, the designer for *42nd Street*, had a scale model built. Santo Loquasto, who did *The Matchmaker* and *Much Ado About Nothing*, used hand-drawn sketches over a floor plan. Robert Brill gave them the 3D computer images. These various visions all become concrete in the set-building shop, located in premises on Brunswick Street that also house the Archives, the Call Centre and the Costume and Props Warehouse.

In the cavernous space there are pieces of new sets strewn around (a glorious winding staircase) along with whimsical bits of old sets (the fuselage of a plane suspended from the ceiling with a superhero dangling from its underside; a model of the Chrysler Building; a reclining gazelle). A dozen or so carpenters can be seen

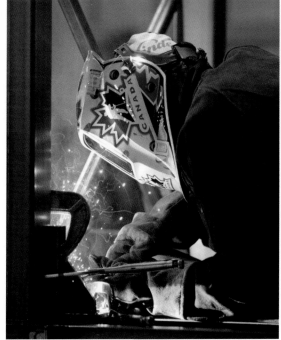

Facing page: Scenic artist Lisa Summers applies gold foil to the eagle created by lead prop builder Ken Dubblestyne for *42nd Street* (2012). Top left: Set model for *42nd Street* by designer Debra Hanson. Top right: Chilina Kennedy (Philia) and Mike Nadajewski (Hero) rehearse with set pieces for *A Funny Thing Happened on the Way to the Forum* (2009). Above left: Scenic carpenter John Roth.

measuring and sawing to the sound of a very loud AC/DC song. Costing the sets began in June, and the actual building started in August. By November four sets were being constructed: *Much Ado About Nothing*, *Henry V*, *42nd Street* and *The Matchmaker*. By January there will be twenty-four carpenters, as deadline pressures begin to mount, and all fourteen sets will be underway.

A complicating factor in repertory theatre is the fact that each theatre houses more than one production at a time. The Festival Theatre will have four shows running on alternate days, with limited storage and a small corridor that connects the stage to the three semi-trailers attached to the building used to store the sets. Everything they build needs to be able to be broken down quickly into pieces that are small enough to get through the corridor (which measures eight feet by nine feet eleven inches) and into the trailers. The set needs to be durable enough to withstand two hundred changeovers, it needs to be light enough to be moved, and it needs to be safe.

It used to be that stagehands would always move pieces during blackouts, but now it's possible to move things mechanically or electronically. This has changed the way pieces are built and how they get on and off the stage, and it changes the way people move, whether it's up through the trap in the floor, or on motorized scenery, or suspended by cables.

Des McAnuff's 2011 production of *Twelfth Night* featured a lot of automation: the motor boat that Viola arrived in, the suspended refrigerator with its opening doors, the cage that rose out of the floor with Malvolio in it. The boat used a wheelchair motor and joystick to propel and steer it. The golf cart that Andrew Aguecheek drove was an actual golf cart, modified by the Festival's artisans. An emergency stop button was installed to kill the power. Making sure an automated piece of scenery can stop is a critical factor.

"There are big red buttons located all over the theatre,"

Mestern says. "Stage management has one; the crew have them backstage. So anyone who sees something going wrong can hit the emergency stop button, and the effect on stage will stop. Everything stops." If a chandelier is being lowered by a winch, or something is rising out of the trap door, those stop too. The platform that rises out of the floor is also monitored by a person below the stage holding a deadman switch that works two ways: if he lets go, it stops, and if he suddenly clenches tightly, it also stops. Human nature is such that in emergency we either clench or let go. Either way, the lift stops.

In *Jesus Christ Superstar*, one of the complexities was Jesus' ascent on the cross at the end. In this stunning effect, a large cross illuminated like a marquee with small light bulbs descended from above at the same time that Jesus (Paul Nolan) was ascending. The two would meet and stop in mid-air so that Jesus, arms spread wide, was framed by the cross behind him. The challenge was how to get Jesus up there.

After considering—and rejecting for safety reasons—the idea of a platform raised by a winch motor and aircraft cable, the automation team settled on a hydraulic lift, with a system of valves that lock. The platform on which Nolan stood was set atop a three-inch-thick mast that could extend eight feet up from the stage. Attached to the apparatus was a drill rod, a length of high-strength three-quarter-inch steel, that rose vertically behind Nolan and was clipped to the belt concealed under his breechcloth. One of the Roman soldiers discreetly hooked him in and also clicked into place two thin horizontal rods on which his arms could rest as he assumed the crucifixion pose. Because the platform was only eighteen inches square and only three-eights of an inch thick, Nolan appeared almost unsupported in his ascension.

Most construction glitches are addressed in rehearsal. Cheney recalls the set for Stratford's 1978 production of *Private Lives*, starring Maggie Smith and Brian Bedford. In

Facing page: In *Twelfth Night*, the musicians moved on motorized platforms. Right: Crew member David Schilz drives the drum-kit platform backstage.

Paul Nolan's Jesus
ascended to the cross
on a hydraulic lift

rehearsal, when the doors on stage slammed, the whole façade shook. "Eventually," Cheney says, "we built the door frames as a separate unit from the scenery."

How something looks on the page or in a computer program isn't always how it looks on stage. "We get feedback from the designer and director once they see it all together on stage," Mestern says. Sometimes the automation doesn't work as expected, or an effect needs to be rethought. "The paint notes come last," Mestern says. "Once the lighting hits the set, they may realize it's too bright or too dark."

In the paint shop the massive floor for *42nd Street* sits, parts of it still waiting to be painted. Various veneers have been tested, using local tap dancers to gauge their durability and the sound quality. The production team are looking for a specific clarity in the tap dancing (and to that end will eventually put microphones in the floor). There also needs to be consistency: a dancer has to sound the same on any part of the stage. Designed to accommodate a specific number of dancers, the floor is essentially a puzzle joined by rotor locks that comes apart to be stored between shows.

The challenge posed by *42nd Street* was the balcony on which a fifteen-piece orchestra plays. "We have to bridge a large area of twelve feet with this orchestra," says Andrew Mestern, "and there's a grand piano up there. It's structural engineering." One of the things they did to lighten the load was gut a grand piano and insert a working electronic keyboard. Steel beams provide the support for the balcony; again, the engineering challenge posed by the repertory system was to make them so they could come apart—and be reassembled— quickly and with relative ease.

Meanwhile, the set-building carpenters are also working on the Festival's fifth theatre space: the Studio Theatre Annex, which will have seventy-five seats and will house two special events: a production of Michael Hollingsworth's *The War of 1812*, performed by Toronto's VideoCabaret company, and a series of late-night cabarets hosted by actor Lucy Peacock in celebration of her twenty-fifth season at Stratford.

Facing page: Thin steel rods (just visible in this close-up view) provided support for Paul Nolan's arms in the crucifixion scene from *Jesus Christ Superstar*. Above: Alternate property master Rory Feore tests the automated motor boat used in the opening scene of *Twelfth Night* (2011).

Above left: Scenic artist Blair Yeomans works from photographs of actor Chilina Kennedy and the real-life Eva Perón to create a portrait used on stage in *Evita* (2010). Above right: Sections of the stage floor designed by Debra Hanson for *As You Like It* (2010). Facing page: A corner of the paint shop.

Top: Designer Santo Loquasto (left) presents his design for the set of *Much Ado About Nothing* (2012) to the construction team. Above left: Scenic artist Kevin Kemp works on the floor for *Much Ado About Nothing*. Above right: Part of the ornate railing for the *Much Ado About Nothing* staircase.

The Brunswick Street building is also where the Festival's vast collection of properties is stored. Distinctions between props, sets and costumes aren't always as clear-cut as audiences might suppose: in addition to such obvious items as scrolls and daggers, props can encompass things as diverse as armour, trees, rugs, drapes, handbags, parasols, furniture and tablecloths. The gigantic staircase-mounted eagle on which the god Jupiter makes his appearance in 2012's *Cymbeline* is considered a prop, not a set piece.

Dona Hrabluk, Head of Properties, starts preparing for the season in September, nine months before opening; the others in her department—located in the basement of the Festival Theatre—usually begin work in November. Collectively, these twelve people possess an astonishing range of talents and skills, from such specialties as sculpting, welding and upholstery to simply having the patience to hand-string ten thousand beads for a chandelier.

The department has an extensive database with photographs of past props, their dimensions and the productions they were used in, and some of those props are re-used. When rehearsals begin, one of the first things Hrabluk does is go to the Costume and Props Warehouse on Brunswick Street, pull whatever is needed, organize it by show and get it ready to be picked up and taken to rehearsal.

What can't be found in the warehouse has to be bought or scrounged or manufactured—and here creativity has to be matched with innovative thinking. What do you use for palm leaves in *Jesus Christ Superstar*? Vinyl, which is durable enough to be repeatedly trampled on. Where do you find 1970s teak furniture for Michel Tremblay's *Hosanna*? Kijiji. The 1928 Chevy truck for *The Grapes of Wrath*? Online. Häagen-Dazs containers for *Twelfth Night*? Buy them on sale at three for $5 and eat the ice cream. The grand piano shell for *42nd Street* came from Jennifer in Box Office, who was trying to get rid of hers.

Often a production will require props that are utterly unique. "We make a lot of prototypes," says Hrabluk.

The floor for *42nd Street* divided into its component pieces.

115

Left and facing page: Prop builder Dylan Mundy works on the *Much Ado About Nothing* staircase. Top right: Designer Santo Loquasto's set model for *Much Ado About Nothing*.

"An eagle on a staircase isn't something you can buy off the shelf. We're making exploding tomato cans for *The Matchmaker*. We made a Victorian paddle wheel for *The Pirates of Penzance*. This is stuff we have to build because it simply doesn't exist elsewhere." In many cases—but not all—designers will provide detailed sketches for props. "Other times," says Hrabluk, "it's a collaboration between the builder and the designer and myself. We do background research and try things out to see if they will work."

Sometimes a prop doesn't work, aesthetically or literally. (At first, the torches in *Jesus Christ Superstar* wouldn't stay lit for the duration of their scene.) The prop builders tinker and re-invent and replace. There is a flurry of adjustment and last-minute change, then a calm when the show opens. Then most of the department leaves for the season, waiting for November to return and do it all again.

Sets, like everything else in theatre, are ephemeral. The experience lasts, but not the physical objects. Some sets will extend their natural lifespan by going on tour or being rented to other companies, and so they need to be broken down into sections that will load into a semi-trailer. *Jesus Christ Superstar* went to California then to New York; *Twelfth Night* was shipped to Australia.

A few iconic pieces will go to the Archives. Some pieces sit in a second Festival warehouse for a while with the hope they will be re-used, but there is only so much space and it's expensive to store them. Occasionally, parts of a set go to a high school drama department. Ultimately, most sets have to be scrapped.

The giant revolve from *Camelot* was kept, but the rest of the floor was thrown out. The houses from *A Funny Thing Happened on the Way to the Forum* all went, as did the beautiful *Tempest* set. All that ingenuity and craftsmanship had to be abandoned; there is no viable way to preserve it. The hardware is stripped off, the steel sold for scrap, and whatever can't be recycled goes into a nearby landfill. And there the discarded sets are overseen by those two veterans of the theatre, Clara and Barb, the hawks from *Camelot*.

Lead prop builder Ken Dubblestyne working on the tree for *Camelot*.

Top: Ken Dubblestyne works on Ariel's harpy wings for *The Tempest* (2010). Above left: Prop builder Michelle Jamieson uses a stencil to paint patterns on fabric for *Camelot*. Above right: Prop builder Heather Ruthig works on pear trees for *Camelot*.

Left: Ken Dubblestyne and Head of Properties Dona Hrabluk. Right: Prop for *As You Like It* (2010).

Specialists Who Do It All

"Carolyn does great food," says Head of Properties Dona Hrabluk—but she's not talking about haute cuisine. Like each of the craftspeople who work in the props department, Carolyn Horley has her own special area of artistry: in her case, the creation of fake food so realistic that even up close it tempts you to take a bite.

Another example is lead builder Ken Dubblestyne, who is particularly renowned for his talent as a sculptor. And props themselves fall into various special categories; among others, these include paper props (parchments, letters, newspapers, magazines etc.) and soft props (cushions, curtains, heraldic banners).

Yet every specialist in the department also has to be able to turn his or her hand to whatever a particular season demands. "Someone who does upholstery in this department can also be a welder," says Hrabluk, with evident pride. "We have a lot of amazing artists here."

Prop builder Carolyn Horley puts the finishing touches on faux desserts.

Facing page: Ken Dubblestyne applies gold paint to a large foam prop for *As You Like It* (2010). Top: A collection of fibreglass helmets. Above left: These devilled eggs by Carolyn Horley are made of plaster mixed with paint. Above right: The giant Styrofoam apple designed by Debra Hanson for *As You Like It* (2010).

Top left: Prop builder Eric Ball repaints chandeliers for *The Matchmaker* (2012). These items have been reused many times since they were made in the 1970s. Above left: Tombstone for *Twelfth Night* (2011). Right: Prop builder Heather Ruthig paints a fire hydrant for *You're a Good Man, Charlie Brown* (2012). Facing page: Prop builders' work stations are creatively crammed with reference materials, mementos and *objets trouvés*. This is Dylan Mundy's tool box.

Notes and Asides:

The Festival Archives:
A Living Legacy

It is a typical day at the Stratford Shakespeare Festival Archives. Paul Thompson and Alon Nashman, the creators of 2012's *Hirsch*, along with designer Gillian Gallow, have dropped by to look at costumes, photos, videos and reviews from John Hirsch's Stratford productions. A magnificent Desmond Heeley robe hangs on a judy (an adjustable torso-shaped form used by dressmakers) in the middle of the reading room. Director of Education Andrea Jackson is looking at photographs and reviews from Gilbert and Sullivan productions. Actors from the Birmingham Conservatory for Classical Theatre—the Festival's in-house training program—are in the media room watching the archival recording of a past Festival show. Head of Properties Dona Hrabluk and her team are looking for crowns for one of the 2012 productions. The Festival's digital media team is scouting locations for promotional photo and video shoots.

A student volunteer is working in the meeting room, identifying actors in early photos. Archivists Christine Schindler and Nora Polley are running around the ten-thousand-square-foot space finalizing selections of costumes and other materials for the new Festival Exhibition opening in downtown Stratford. Dr. Francesca Marini, a leading performing arts archivist with international experience who became the new Archives Director in 2010, is showing around a visitor who has turned up asking for a tour.

The Archives is open year-round and there is never a downtime. More than sixteen hundred people—from individual patrons to tour groups large and small—come through the door each year. Requests pour in every day from Festival staff and company members, as well as from outside users. The phone rings: the Publicity Department is asking for photos for the press. A scholar emails to arrange an extended visit to study the work of Jean Gascon,

---

Facing page: Part of the 2011 Archives Tours display. Right: Costume designed by Tanya Moiseiwitsch and worn by Alec Guinness as Richard III in the Festival's inaugural production in 1953. In the background are binders of press clippings from the pre-digital age.

a former Festival Artistic Director and one of the founders of the National Theatre School; a group of university graduate students wants materials for a course project; a professor wants to bring students to Archives for a teaching session and research; a theatre producer wants images for a William Shatner one-man show; an audio-visual consultant is inquiring about photos for a Christopher Plummer documentary; a donor wants to give the Archives her precious collection of Desmond Heeley's original costume designs.

Housed in the same Brunswick Street building as the scene shop, a few blocks south of the Festival Theatre, this is one of the largest and most complete performing arts archives in the world—and is considered the largest devoted to a single theatre. Its holdings date back to the Festival's founding in 1952.

Every production since the first season in 1953 is documented in some way: through stage managers' scripts, directors' notes, music, design bibles, original design sketches, technical drawings, costumes (at least two or three per show), props and even pieces of scenery, plus reviews and press clippings. Thousands of photographs of productions, actors and events are complemented by a huge audio-visual collection, including archival video recordings of every production since 1968.

The earliest of them is *Romeo and Juliet*, with the young Christopher Walken. There are King Henrys, Richards, Lears, Portias, Shylocks, Hamlets, Titanias, Pucks, Juliets—and William Hutt majestically furred and feather-hatted as Lady Bracknell in *The Importance of Being Earnest*. There is a *Much Ado About Nothing* set in the 1920s and a *Two Gentlemen of Verona* with hockey gear. A few earlier productions are represented by brief clips, showcasing such famous actors as Alan Bates, who played Richard III in 1967.

The Archives also houses a rare copy of the Fourth Folio of Shakespeare's works and a chair believed to have been owned by Shakespeare himself. Less glamorously, but of no less importance, there are documents from each administrative department: legal records, contracts, correspondence, marketing materials, minutes from board meetings, box-office reports. As Marini puts it, "The Festival's legacy and accountability largely reside in the Archives."

Left: Roy Brown, former Head of Properties for the Avon and Tom Patterson theatres, restores set models for the 2012 Festival Exhibition. Facing page, top: Archives Director Francesca Marini (left) and Head of Properties Dona Hrabluk. Right: Sculptural pieces designed by Darko Tresnjak for his production of *Titus Andronicus* (2011). Far right: Costume sketch by Robert Perdziola for Falstaff in *The Merry Wives of Windsor* (2011).

Chapter Six

The Art of Wearable Storytelling

Gerry Altenburg, who is Head of Wigs and Makeup, once followed a man around Stratford's Canadian Tire store. The man was a large biker with a white beard and long white hair, and Altenburg coveted that hair. "I was kind of afraid," he recalls, "because he was a big guy. But I said, 'Excuse me, I don't want to sound too forward, but I work at the theatre and I do wigs. If you ever cut your hair off, please let me know.'" And he gave the man his card.

"Two years later, he called me. He came over to my house and I gave him a haircut. Some of that hair ended up in Christopher Plummer's toupée for *Barrymore*. It was just such a perfect colour. It's hard to find." He chuckles at the thought: "Barrymore with biker hair."

Most wigs at Stratford are made from human hair. Musicals are an exception: about half of the wigs used in them are synthetic, because of the physicality of musical theatre and the extra upkeep it entails. (Perspiration, for instance, tends to be more of an issue in musicals.) Synthetics are also stretchier than custom-made wigs with real hair and can thus more easily accommodate the microphones that are used in musical theatre. But even the synthetic wigs are customized to make them look more natural.

The Festival buys its hair from merchants in England who travel throughout Europe and Asia collecting it; Russia and Italy are big suppliers. Hair quality depends on diet and hygiene. Over-washed hair is less appealing to wigmakers; natural oils make for better lustre.

"Usually what we buy is called virgin hair," Altenburg says. "You can tell when you've got something that's

Head of Wigs and Makeup Gerry Altenburg.

Top: Head of Wigs and Makeup Gerry Altenburg dresses a wig for Chilina Kennedy to wear as Lois Lane in *Kiss Me, Kate* (2010). Above left: Tracy Frayne works on knotting a wig. Above right: Wigmaker Lorna Henderson with one of the more than eight hundred wigs that are stored at the Festival Theatre. Facing page: Dressing (i.e., styling) wigs is an art in itself. This wig was worn by Ben Carlson as Alceste in *The Misanthrope* (2011).

been over-processed: it's a bit too soft and difficult to work with."

Over the years, the department has built up a large stock of wigs that can be altered and reused. The twelve shows in the 2011 season used 242 wigs, eighty percent of them from existing stock. After use, wigs are washed, rinsed and conditioned, then filed by colour and length. More than eight hundred of them are stored in the Festival Theatre, where such perennial stars as Seana McKenna have their own designated drawers full of wigs from past seasons that they can wear again when the need arises. There is also a concrete-lined fire-retardant cabinet for facial hair, which comes—to many people's surprise—from the tails and bellies of yaks.

The wig season starts in late autumn, when the department first gets a sense of what the next season's productions will look like. "Then in December," says Altenburg, "I start working with designers on the actual show. I meet with the designers and directors, then in January we start work on creating the wigs." Designers don't usually provide specific wig sketches; instead the wigmakers work from the costume designs and from their discussions with the director and designer.

There are wigs in almost every production at Stratford, and they are custom-fitted for each actor. "The first thing we have to do," Altenburg says, "is capture the shape of the actor's head and hairline." This is done with plastic wrap—the same food-storage film found in most kitchen drawers—which is carefully wrapped around the actor's head and then covered with transverse strips of ordinary adhesive tape. "Then you draw around the hairline, you pull it off, and you have an accurate and surprisingly rigid form that can be used over and over again. It's very low-tech, but it yields an accurate result."

That form is then tried out on various-sized "blocks" (head shapes made of wood) until one is found that it fits. The wig's lace foundation—a fine mesh that becomes almost invisible when laid against the skin—is then formed on that block by means of hand-sewn folds and pleats of the utmost delicacy.

Facing page: A selection of the department's work. Above left: Facial hair used by the Festival comes from a surprising source: the bellies and tails of yaks. Above right: An extreme example of the wigmaker's art, worn by Robert Persichini as Montfleury in *Cyrano de Bergerac* (2009).

The materials and tools involved in wigmaking haven't changed much over the centuries. "We have knotting hooks for tying hair," Altenburg says, "and we have an apparatus with a succession of strings that we can weave hair in and out of, and you end up with weft. It creates a product that a lot of people use in their hair extensions."

In one day, an actor may be playing two or more characters who have very different hair

On average, it takes a week to build a single wig. "Once the foundation is fitted and we've drawn the hair line, it goes to a knotter who ties in the hair. In the front, at the hairline, one hair is knotted at a time. As you work away from the hairline, it's two, three, four hairs at a time. It's like miniature rug-hooking. When I started in this business, I thought I'd never be able to do it. Your eyes are so focused on the work; mine were watering after my very first hour. But eventually it becomes quite relaxing."

When you see the actors' headshots in the lobby, you wonder: why not just use the actor's own (sometimes luxurious) hair? But putting that hair up in rollers and styling it into whatever shape it needs to be for the show can take up to an hour for each actor, and there aren't nearly enough hair people working each show for that to be possible.

And there is the challenge of working in repertory: in one day the actor may be playing two or more characters who have very different hair. Paul Nolan, who played Jesus in *Jesus Christ Superstar*, wanted to use his own hair. But he was also appearing in *The Grapes of Wrath*, where his character required far less hair than Jesus. There was a further complication. When Jesus' clothes were yanked off near the end of the show, he still had to

Above: Wigmaker Erica Croft-Fraser preps Paul Nolan's own hair prior to fitting his wig for *Jesus Christ Superstar*. Facing page: Tom Patterson Theatre Department Head Julie Scott applies a bald pate to Seana McKenna for her performance in the title role of *Richard III* (2011).

Above and facing page: Seana McKenna's transformation into Richard III continues, with the help of Julie Scott.

Above and facing page: Avon Theatre Department Head Teddi Barrett helps Gareth Potter undergo his transformation into the title character of *Hosanna* (2011).

have a microphone pack. Wearing it in his loincloth was ruled out because the wire would be visible up his back. So it had to be in his hair; he had to wear a wig.

"There is a level of discomfort when wearing a wig," Altenburg says, "so some actors dislike wearing them. Others love the idea of changing their appearance."

Ideally, he wants to have the wigs completed a week to two weeks before the dress rehearsal, so that the designers can see them in their finished, dressed state. By then, fittings have been carried out, necessary adjustments have been made, and the colour has been perfectly blended. Altenburg tries to get the actor in some version of his or her costume when they are doing a wig fitting. "If they're being fitted for an Elizabethan-style wig and they show up in shorts and running shoes and a T-shirt that says Led Zeppelin on it, it's hard to visualize the total effect."

Roughly half of the fifteen people in the department also do makeup. With advances in lighting, theatrical makeup and street makeup have become closer in style and product over the years. What hasn't changed is the need for prosthetics and other special makeup effects, such as false noses, scars and even occasionally teeth. Stage blood, which always has to be handled carefully to prevent it from spreading onto costumes and the surface of the stage, is a shared responsibility. "Blood is a combination of us and Props," says Altenburg. "The dividing line is, if it's on the actor, then it's makeup. If it's coming out of a trick knife, it's a prop."

Altenburg, who has worked in other theatres across North America, as well as on film sets, can speak with some authority when he calls the Festival's commitment to the arts of wigmaking and makeup "second to none"—a sentiment echoed by artisans in other departments too. Stratford is the only theatre in North America that has the capacity to manufacture all its own wigs, costumes, shoes, sets and props. Only the Metropolitan Opera Company in New York can rival it.

Left: Milliner Isabel Bloor with a selection of headgear.
Facing page: Cutter Carol A. Miller works on a costume.

The Stratford Shakespeare Festival is the only theatre in North America that has the capacity to manufacture all its own wigs, costumes, shoes and props.

The design aesthetic established by Stratford's founding designer, Tanya Moiseiwitsch, called for great finesse and attention to detail.

In part, this is a result of Stratford's relative isolation. Instead of importing from Toronto or New York or London, it was cheaper for the Festival to make its own costumes, props and wigs. Also, the design aesthetic established by Stratford's founding designer, Tanya Moiseiwitsch, called for great finesse and attention to detail, simply because the Festival Theatre's thrust stage configuration puts the audience so close to the action. As a result, Stratford's theatrical craftspeople became among the best on the continent. What was born of necessity, says General Director Antoni Cimolino, became a virtue. It meant that costumes could be tailored specifically to the needs of a show, that they could contribute thematically to what the director wanted to express.

"Everything on the Stratford Festival stage is made to tell a specific story that the director and the designer and the actors in rehearsals have decided on," says Cimolino. "In many theatres the designers are reduced to buyers: go out and buy what you need. If we were to use a costume shop, and you wanted, say, 1850s military clothes from Bulgaria, you'd go to a costume store and they'd have it on the rack. Whereas at Stratford, we build everything for that designer and that actor to tell the story. So if they want to do a fantasy on it, or make it short and funny-looking, they can. We do the patterns specifically for the actor's body based on the story we're telling. We have the only shop in North America where we not only dye things but paint them. And that's driven by necessity."

Over the years, Stratford has amassed an extraordinary collection of costumes that its artisans have built, most of them stored in the Brunswick Street warehouse. The racks of suits, dresses, togas, armour and uniforms have become, in effect, the Festival's own costume shop. Pieces from that collection are not only re-used (usually modified) but also rented out to other theatres.

Designer Carolyn M. Smith has worked at Stratford for fourteen seasons, most recently designing costumes for *The Grapes of Wrath* in 2011 and *Cymbeline* in 2012. She starts in the summer, a year before the play opens, first reading the script and, in consultation with the

Facing page: Rebecca Dillow, of the Bijoux/Decoration Department, works on a costume for *Peter Pan* (2010) Above: Designer Carolyn M. Smith at the Costume and Props Warehouse.

Top: Designer Paul Tazewell and cutter Johanna Billings in a costume fitting for *The Tempest* (2010).
Above left: Tazewell's design sketch for Juno in *The Tempest*. Above right: The Wardrobe Department's work encompasses not only items of clothing ranging from millinery to boots and shoes but also bijoux (jewellery).

director, getting a sense of the play and the period. She then creates sketches on her computer, prints them out and makes collages. Once she knows what she wants, she checks to see what she can use from stock, from the vast collection in the Costume Warehouse.

"When I first started, I had to use everything from stock," she says. "Most designers use stock now. We were trying to find men's jeans for *The Grapes of Wrath*. We bought jeans, then we found some in the warehouse more appropriate to the period. To make them look old, we had to make holes and patch them, then dye them to look yellowed and dirty."

The costume people get the designs in October, working a full season ahead. What usually follows is a month of back-and-forth over budget. If a designer's proposals prove too expensive to build, says Design Coordinator Alix Dolgoy, "then I start going out to the warehouse and looking at what's there and making suggestions."

Dolgoy has been at Stratford for twenty seasons, working first on musicals, then on Shakespeare. "I like the research behind it," she says. "Shakespeare is so freeing for a designer: you can do it as it's described in the text, because he does describe so much, or you can do it in a way that's been done before, or you can think of a new way and mix it all up." Designers do exhaustive research on the period, the context, the social history, in order to understand what clothes people wore and why they wore them.

The Wardrobe Department interprets the sketches that come from the designer and negotiates the large, lightly charted territory between the designer's intention, the budget and the actor's needs. Once the budgets are signed off, the next step is to start looking at fabrics. The designer or an assistant designer and a cutter buy the fabrics in late fall, finding some of them locally and ordering others from Germany, England and the U.S., using catalogues that have swatches in them. By January they've started building. There are fittings in February, and everything has to be ready by the technical dress rehearsal in spring.

Left: Assistant costume designer Sara Brzozowski (left) and costume designer Carolyn M. Smith look for ruffs for *Cymbeline* (2012). Right: Assistant set designer Devon Bhim with the floor plan for *Much Ado About Nothing* (2012).

Top: Set designer Scott Penner with the set model for *Cymbeline* (2012). Above left: Rolls of fabric are stored in an area known as "the cage." Above right: Items from the Bijoux/Decoration Department. Facing page: Design Coordinator Alix Dolgoy and designer Santo Loquasto do research for *The Matchmaker* (2012).

"No one else does costumes like we do," says Anne Moore, the Wardrobe Manager. When Moore gets the designs in October, she has to figure out what staff will be necessary to build them. Her job includes hiring millinery apprentices, wardrobe apprentices, setting up sewing tests for new sewers and doing the time sheets for the dressers and wigmakers who are already on the job. "Craftspeople are added later," she says, "but the cutters come in within two weeks, and we stagger the sewers. Each team builds about five or six costumes. Each cutter works on three shows." There are 126 people in the Wardrobe Department: sewers, cutters, buyers, dyers, milliners, jewellery wranglers, shoemakers, maintenance people. It is a small corporation that requires a great deal of organization and political adroitness.

The work that goes into building Festival costumes is incredibly rigorous. Not only do their details have to be convincing and authentic for audiences with such a vivid close-up view, they also need to be extraordinarily well constructed because of the stress on them. "Especially musicals," says Moore. "The action is frantic; the quick changes cause incredible stress to costumes. Zippers have to be reinforced, as they're yanked on. The trim has to be sewn on really well so an actor doesn't catch his heel in it and injure himself."

Costumes that are bought usually don't last, but the ones that are made are usually re-used over the years. The department has costumes from the 1950s that are still in good shape. Newly built costumes can look oddly flat under stage lighting, so they are sometimes painted to give them more texture and make them look lived-in and natural.

"For the actor," says Bruce Dow, "the icing on the cake is getting to work with the amazing craftspeople at Stratford, to work with the wigmakers, the hat-makers, the shoemakers, the cutters who put the wardrobe together. Having a costume fitting shows you why this place is special. You're standing there in your knickers with between ten and fifteen people, and a designer and a design assistant working over you. They come in

Facing page: Designer Desmond Heeley in a fitting with Sara Topham (Gwendolen Fairfax) for *The Importance of Being Earnest* (2009). Above: Designer Paul Tazewell in the Costume and Props Warehouse.

Left: Not a costume but a prop. Prop builder Shirley Lee works on the huge cloth that covered the stage at the start of *As You Like It* (2010). Right: Victoria Shillington sews a pair of pants. Facing page: Chris Molhoughney and Connie Puetz of the Boots and Shoes Department.

Top left: Spools of thread are carefully organized by colour. Top right: These costume-builders' forms are known as "judies." Above: Cutter Johanna Billings works on a costume for *Jesus Christ Superstar* (2011). Facing page: Company member Jonathan Purdon with designer John Pennoyer in a fitting for *The Winter's Tale* (2010).

and talk to you about your feet and ask what physically you are doing in the role, and they adjust your costume to accommodate that. Every hat is made to fit your head like a glove."

One of the most famous designers (of both costumes and sets) in Stratford's history is Desmond Heeley, who began his career as a design assistant on Peter Brook's 1955 production of *Titus Andronicus* at the Shakespeare Memorial Theatre in Stratford, England. That restrained interpretation (only the second time that Shakespeare's bloodiest play had been staged in a century) starred Laurence Olivier and Vivien Leigh and was heralded as a breakthrough.

"Jesus' disappearing suit had tiny magnets holding it together"

Heeley first came to Stratford, Ontario, in 1957 to design *Hamlet*, which starred Christopher Plummer. It was the first Stratford production that wasn't designed by Tanya Moiseiwitsch, the British designer who created the theatre's thrust stage. Heeley, a disciple of Moiseiwitsch, went on to do dozens of productions at Stratford, and some of his exquisite costumes and masks can be seen in the Festival Archives. He was a meticulous designer—he liked to see an actor work before designing a costume specifically for him—and set the bar for designers who came after.

Some costumes need to be specially designed for a particular effect, like Jesus' disappearing suit in *Jesus Christ Superstar*. Near the end of the show, Paul Nolan's Jesus would be standing on a ramp in an outfit that suddenly and dramatically disappeared, leaving him in his crucifixion loincloth. The suit was yanked off his body and down through a hole in the stage floor; the challenge was to make it happen fast enough that

it would look like the suit was simply vanishing.

"It took a lot of thinking," says Anne Moore. "It had tiny magnets holding it together. Someone in the trap would pull it and the magnets would fly apart and the suit disappeared. Velcro would have made too much noise and it would grab on itself. Two mock-ups were made before it finally worked. We changed fabrics because the first one was too textured and grabbed going down the hole."

Making costumes for quick changes poses a similar challenge. You need to know if there are quick changes before you build a costume, because then it has to be designed with, say, a thirty-second change in mind. "Thirty seconds is a fast change," Moore says. "A very fast change. In *A Funny Thing Happened on the Way to the Forum*, the Eunuchs had a *five*-second change. It was also done with magnets." Moore initially got the idea from a television commercial in which someone walked through a screen door that had magnets in it and it snapped back into place instantly.

"About a month before we are ready for tech dress," says Alix Dolgoy, "this room gets really frenetic, and that's when you say, 'Oh my God, it's never going to be done, it's never going to look good—never, never, never.' Then it all comes together."

Getting 126 people moving in concert to accommodate the vision of ten or more directors and designers while dealing with the idiosyncrasies of hundreds of actors is a task that requires a gift not only for craftsmanship but also for organization and diplomacy. The department also serves as a training ground: hundreds of people have worked at Stratford and gone on to other theatres in the country.

"I really believe that Stratford is Canada's national theatre," says Dolgoy, "and we have a responsibility to train people to work in this level of theatre. It's the only theatre in the country where we work at this level. Most of the designers working in the country have come through here. It's sort of a benchmark. It's where a lot of them got their start, where they learned how to design a show."

Chapter Seven

The Sound (and Light) of Music

"In our production of *Jesus Christ Superstar*," says Stratford's Director of Music, Rick Fox, "we added the song 'Could We Start Again Please,' which was written for the movie. We changed it up a bit. In the movie it was sung by Mary and Peter with a full chorus, and it looks a bit like a Pepsi commercial. So we cut the ensemble vocals, and Des came up with the brilliant idea of bringing Judas in to sing a part of it.

"We were terrified about what Andrew Lloyd Webber would say about us doing that. First of all, he's notorious for not allowing any changes to his work. The reason is, he was twenty-three when the first Broadway production was mounted. He was not the famous Andrew Lloyd Webber at that point and did not have as much artistic clout as he would have liked. He was very critical of the production, and legend has it that on opening night he vowed to create his own production company so he could control his work and never have that happen again.

"So we were nervous about it—but he came to see it and absolutely loved it. The phone rang in the pit and the stage manager said, 'Lord Lloyd Webber's on his way to the pit.' When he got there, he said, 'I don't think I've ever heard it played better.'"

Fox, who has been the Festival's Director of Music since 2007, grew up playing classical piano, then got interested in rock and roll, before studying jazz in New York. In addition to his other responsibilities, he usually

Guitarist Kevin Ramessar (left) and Director of Music Rick Fox in the orchestra pit at the Avon Theatre during a performance of *Jesus Christ Superstar*. Behind them can be seen audience members sitting in the front row.

acts as musical director and conductor for at least one of the season's musical productions.

"On a basic level," he says, "musical direction is executing the music. It starts with casting, getting the right voices. I'm often involved before the director, weeding out people who simply don't have the technical ability for the roles. The casting director will do a wave of general auditions and whittle it down to a smaller number. Then I'll come in and whittle it further, along with the choreographer, if it's a dance show. Increasingly, performers are expected to be very proficient at both."

Once the cast is assembled, the musical director has the job of teaching the music to the performers. "I always start teaching them the song exactly as written," says Fox, "and then we may want to make changes to suit the actor. But you want to base it on what the writers wrote."

Fox's responsibilities extend to everything musical at the Festival, from composing, conducting, directing and casting to the Monday-night concerts in the Festival Theatre lobby. "I oversee all the music," he says, "but I have two or three projects that are mine specifically, then I help steer the guest composers or guest musical directors for other projects. In June you're doing auditions for the next year. In late fall you put the season together: you contract who you need, getting the composers we need, the back-and-forth with budget numbers, maybe we need an extra musician here or there. In January we gear up for rehearsals, then we open."

During the season, Fox conducts the shows he is directly working on and makes sure the others run smoothly. Unlike actors, musicians aren't understudied; if they are sick or need to miss a performance for any other reason, they have to find a replacement themselves and ensure that he or she is proficient. The most important aspect of Fox's job has nothing to do with music, he says. "Diplomacy! How to get along with people and work with them and figure out what their problems are, what they want, why they maybe can't have it. Diplomacy is key."

Facing page: The orchestra loft at the Festival Theatre.
Right: Director of Music Rick Fox at his home in Stratford.

Top: Director of Music Rick Fox conducting a performance of *Camelot*. Left: Horn player Kate Stone during a performance of *Camelot*. Right: Guitarist Kevin Ramessar during a performance of *Jesus Christ Superstar*.

Last year Fox was musical director on two very different shows—*Jesus Christ Superstar* and *Camelot*—that required very different skills. *Camelot* was one of the last of the big stage musicals to be written in a traditional style. Those musicals had a cultural impact beyond their stage runs because, prior to the 1960s, their songs were often the pop hits of the day. That trend was eroded by early rock and roll and then finally swept away entirely by the Beatles. *Jesus Christ Superstar* was one of the first rock expressions of that musical form, following *Hair* (1967) and The Who's *Tommy* (which was released as a double album in 1969 but didn't become a stage show until 1992, when Des McAnuff produced and directed it at La Jolla).

Newer musicals use different instrumentation and require very different voices

The evolution of the musical was a function of culture, economics and technology. The original casts of shows like *Camelot* were huge. Along with the principals, there would be fourteen to sixteen singers and fourteen dancers. In the days before amplification, more voices were needed to make an impact. With amplification, that was no longer necessary. And as the economics of stage musicals shifted, producers could no longer afford a cast of forty people. The ensemble was pared down drastically, and the singers had to dance. Instead of thirty singers and dancers, there were eight or ten actors who could do both. The original version of *42nd Street* was written for forty-four people; the Stratford version has twenty-five.

Jesus Christ Superstar was a response to the traditional musical form. It was louder, yet also more intimate. Because the singers were amplified, the music

Music Administrator and keyboardist Marilyn Dallman during a performance of *Jesus Christ Superstar*.

could play behind them rather than in between. It meant that the leads had to be singers—very good singers. With *Camelot*, Lerner and Loewe wrote the score for an actor. Though Richard Burton could carry a tune (thanks, perhaps, to his Welsh heritage), he wasn't really a singer. But the songs that Arthur sings don't require a great range. The part of Jesus, on the other hand, requires both an operatic range and a rock-and-roll sensibility.

Shows from fifty years ago were longer, in part because the audiences had longer attention spans but also for technical reasons. Sometimes a song was inserted simply to cover for a scene change. Two characters stood in front of the curtain, filling time while the scene was being changed behind them.

The difference between the two musical styles dictates different ways of producing the plays. The orchestra for Stratford's *Camelot* was a robust twenty-six, while the much louder *Jesus Christ Superstar* needed only eleven. There were different amplification needs, and they required very different voices. Newer musicals use different instrumentation and also make more demands on the sound system. "Sound was a big challenge," Fox says. "Four years ago we couldn't have done *Superstar* because we didn't have the sound equipment to do it. It would have sounded awful. The old system was designed for *The Music Man* or Gilbert and Sullivan. But it couldn't carry the weight of rock music."

Evita, which Stratford produced in 2010, was the Festival's first foray into electric rock musicals. A new sub-woofer system was installed for that show. For both *Evita* and *Jesus Christ Superstar* the drums were taken out of the orchestra pit and put into a glass-walled room down the hall. The bass player was in a separate room and a percussionist in yet another room. This allowed them to produce the volume needed for the score without overwhelming all the other musicians in the pit. All the musicians wore headphones. The keyboards

Left: For *Jesus Christ Superstar*, bassist Kevin Muir plays in a separate room. Facing page: Clarinettist Ian Harper in the orchestra pit of the Avon Theatre.

were silent in the pit—the sound came out of the headphones and the house speakers. "If you put all of that band into the pit," says Fox. "It would be chaos. This way, it's like a recording studio."

In theatre, there is the music and there is the sound, two related but distinct entities. Fox takes care of the music, but there are sound designers who deal with the increasing complexity of the actual sound. They are the ones who deliver the music to the audience. "The sound designers have a huge impact on our work," Fox says. "I work very closely with them and I enjoy that—we have some wonderful sound designers here. It's a funny, symbiotic relationship, because everything we do goes through the sound design and if you're not working together, you're not going to get good results."

The Greek amphitheatre near the village of Epidaurus is one of the best preserved in the country. Built in the fourth century BC, it was covered by earth until the late nineteenth century when it was excavated, showing thirty-four rows of stone seats (to which the ancient Romans had added another twenty-one). The acoustics remain remarkable: a person standing on stage can be clearly heard nearly two hundred feet away. This clarity is thought to be the result of the material and dimensions of the limestone seats, which act as an acoustic filter, suppressing low-frequency sound—the major component of background noise—while helping transmit the higher frequencies of the actors' voices.

The Roman architect Vitruvius (80 BC–15 BC) noted the extraordinary acoustics of the Greek amphitheatres. "By the rules of mathematics and the method of music [the Greeks] sought to make the voices from the stage rise more clearly and sweetly to the spectators' ears . . . by the arrangement of theatres in accordance with the science of harmony, the ancients increased the power of the voice."

Those lessons didn't last, however. The history of theatre acoustics is a war of sorts, one that isn't always won by musicians or actors. The Globe theatre in Shakespeare's

London had famously bad acoustics. The actors had to shout to be heard. There are modern theatres in which actors still have to shout. While there are concert spaces like the Four Seasons Centre for Performing Arts in Toronto that are built around beautiful acoustics, too often the acoustics are an afterthought that must accommodate the architecture. While theatre acoustics are evolving, sound itself is undergoing a revolution. Digital technology has changed the game completely.

The last decade has seen the rise of sound design as an integral part of the theatre. The aural experience should be the same for everyone in the audience—a challenge, because just as there are viewing angles, there are listening angles. And there is the added hurdle of the thrust stage at three of the Festival's five theatre spaces.

"Our biggest challenge is the Festival Theatre with its thrust stage," says Peter McBoyle, the Resident Sound Designer, whose job it is to deal with all aspects of sound in any production. Because the actors are essentially placed among the audience members, it makes it difficult to get the sound right. They aren't just projecting forward, as they would with a proscenium stage. To complicate things, the actors' backs are often turned toward some part of the audience.

In a musical, the audience has to hear both the actors and the orchestra, and the actors have to hear themselves, each other and the orchestra. This can also be crucial when music plays a significant role in a non-musical play, as in the 2011 *Twelfth Night*, which had live music on stage, in the form of drums and guitars, as well as a pre-recorded soundtrack: hence the earphones worn by the onstage musicians to keep them in sync.

There are qualitative aspects to the sound as well. As Jim Neil, a sound designer at Stratford, put it, "Is the audience part of the show, or is it perceiving the show?" The answer determines how the sound is distributed throughout the theatre. All of the sound—singers, orchestra, actors, bird noises—has to travel

Left: Resident Sound Designer Peter McBoyle, crew member Michael Duncan and Festival Theatre Head of Sound Scott Matthews with the Festival Theatre main speaker cluster. Facing page: Peter McBoyle in the Avon Theatre.

Rocking the Classics

From the very first season, when Louis Applebaum composed the fanfares for *Richard III* that are still used today to herald performances at the Festival Theatre, music has been a crucial part of the Festival's art.

Other notable composers of original music for Stratford productions include Duke Ellington, who wrote the score for *Timon of Athens* in 1963, and Barenaked Ladies, who scored Antoni Cimolino's production of *As You Like It* in 2005. But it was not until the tenure of Des McAnuff that Stratford could boast an Artistic Director who is also himself a composer.

Music was McAnuff's first artistic love: he performed as a folk singer in his early teens, and at the age of nineteen wrote a rock musical, *Urbania*, that was produced by Toronto's Poor Alex Theatre in 1971. Since then he has composed for many of his own productions, most recently (in collaboration with Michael Roth) his guitars-and-drums-infused *Twelfth Night*. And, of course, his rock-music roots have also helped him win international acclaim for such hits as *The Who's Tommy*, *Jersey Boys* and Stratford's own *Jesus Christ Superstar*.

Des McAnuff performs with the band at an event in his honour at Ryerson University.

throughout the room in uniform waves, and it has to seem as effortless and natural as if we were all in the amphitheatre at Epidaurus.

Just as sound design has become a major part of the theatrical experience, lighting design has grown increasingly complex. The days of someone pointing a spotlight at the actor are decades past, but computers have opened up new possibilities for the subtleties of lighting. Michael Walton is the lighting designer for 2012's *The Matchmaker*, *A Word or Two* and *Henry V*. "Essentially I work with the director and the set designer to create a world," he says. "My job is to create an atmosphere, to shift the focus of the audience or shift the mood of the room, to reinforce what the text gives us. It's done by varying the intensity of light, varying the colours, the placement of the lights. Often the audience isn't really aware of it."

In 2011, Walton worked on *Twelfth Night*, which had 440 lighting cues. The average is between two hundred and three hundred. Some of these are so subtle they're undetectable, while others are overtly dramatic. Faces are lit for emphasis; parts of the stage are highlighted or shaded. Usually the lighting subtly invites our eyes somewhere without us being aware of the invitation.

Walton first reads the play then attends the rehearsals, making notes about each scene. "I'm looking for where the story is," he says. "If there's a battle, for example, you follow the lead character. Everyone needs to be lit, but the lead is more prominent. Then you ask: Is this an early-morning battle? Or is it the middle of the night? Do we want fires on the periphery?"

Walton has an array of lights to produce whatever effect he can imagine. At the Festival Theatre there are three hundred lights up in the rigging, and each production then adds to that, bringing in whatever specific lights it requires, bringing the total to five hundred by season's end. There are accessories called scrollers that can project twenty-four different colours; there are a hundred scrollers at the Festival Theatre. There are lights that can produce any colour on the spectrum. The array of effects is almost limitless.

After Walton chooses what light to use, what colour and intensity and placement he wants for each scene, master electrician Alec Cooper punches the information into a computer. When the show begins its run, every cue is lined up in the computer and is activated by Cooper up in the lighting booth, on commands from the stage manager.

The lighting can range from the symphonic, as it was in *Twelfth Night*, to the simple. But even a one-man show can be deceptively complex. Christopher Plummer's *A Word or Two* has only him on stage, yet the lighting isn't merely a spot that follows him. "We're taking a bit of a journey with Chris," says Walton, who designed the production's lighting. "In the show, he looks at the books that have influenced him, so we're regularly transplanting the audience through literature, and the lighting reflects that."

In the original Globe theatre, the tightly packed afternoon crowd didn't see much lighting other than natural light. In other, indoor Elizabethan theatres, usually in halls, candles were used. Lighting design was restricted to the placement of those candles and replacing the ones that had burned down. Occasionally actors would carry torches to indicate that it was night, but this effect didn't change the actual lighting; it only invited the audience to imagine that it was night.

Sound effects were a bit more sophisticated: musicians were a staple of Elizabethan theatre. It is thought that they played between acts or certain scenes as entertainment, as well as in the play itself. Some of the effects were a risk: cannons were sometimes used to signal an entrance, but it was a spark from a cannon that set the thatched roof of the Globe on fire in 1613, burning down the theatre. Fireworks were used to connote lightning or battle scenes, also a gamble.

What these crude effects shared with the modern wizardry of sound and lighting designers is that they were there to enhance the experience, to stimulate the audience's imagination. To transport us not just to Illyria or Birnam Wood or Verona, but to Hamlet's torment, Lear's anguish, to the mischievous mind of Puck.

Actor and singer Nikki M. James performs at the September 2011 gala in honour of Christopher Plummer. The two played the title roles in Des McAnuff's production of *Caesar and Cleopatra* (2008).

Above and facing page: Lighting designer Michael Walton works on *42nd Street* (2012) at the Festival Theatre. Top left: Master electrician Alec Cooper.

Top left: Part of the lighting array at the Festival Theatre. Top right: The "cupcake" in the Festival Theatre ceiling. Above: Master electrician Alec Cooper working on *42nd Street* (2012). Facing page: From the catwalks above the ceiling, crew member Les MacLean looks down at the theatre's hundreds of lights.

Chapter Eight

Air Traffic Controllers of the Stage

"I did *West Side Story* here in 1999," says Cindy Toushan, who has worked as a stage manager for thirty years, "and it was just crisis control every day. We did 157 performances and had the full company on stage only four times. We did 153 shows with people out. We had separated shoulders, we had broken thumbs, a blocked bowel, emergency surgery. We had a dancer who said he didn't feel well, but we had three people out and so we couldn't send him home. We put pails on each side backstage in case he had to throw up. Half an hour after the show he doubled over and we took him to the hospital and he had his appendix removed. That show was a nightmare."

Many of Shakespeare's plays depict a battle between order and disorder, either in the individual (*Hamlet*) or the state (*Henry V*) or both (*King Lear*). That battle exists offstage in every theatre production. Part of the stage manager's job is to make sure it doesn't happen on stage, that disorder doesn't triumph, and that what the audience sees is no more and no less than the director intended.

The job begins a week before the start of rehearsals (as early as February) and continues throughout the run of the production. Usually each stage manager works on only one show a season, though sometimes they do two if one opens early and the other opens later in the season. In that first week, the stage managers scramble to learn as much as they can about the production they'll be working on. They meet with the

---

In the stage manager's booth, Cynthia Toushan runs a performance of *Camelot*.

director (if available) and the designer, obtain copies of the design sketches, talk to the artisans who are already at work building the costumes and the props. They do more mundane things too: marking out the floor of the rehearsal room with spike tape (adhesive tape that comes in different colours) so the actors can see where the set will be, and ensuring that the room is stocked with water jugs and cups, chairs and boxes of tissues.

The first day of rehearsals can be an intimidating occasion, particularly for an artist new to the company, so it generally begins with a half-hour meet-and-greet. Then the actors sit at a table with their scripts in front of them to read the play aloud together for the first time. The rehearsal period, Toushan says, is a stage manager's busiest time. "We are there before everybody else, and we are there after."

The stage manager's job is to make sure the audience sees what the director intended

Scheduling rehearsals in the spaces available is a complex process. A company that presents only one production at a time might rehearse it for three weeks; at Stratford, where several productions are rehearsed at once (with actors often shared among them), rehearsal time is measured in hours, spread out over a couple of months. A small production, such as 2011's *The Little Years*, might rehearse for about 135 hours prior to technical rehearsals; a large-scale show will take longer.

"The rehearsal process itself is divided into roughly two periods," says Ann Stuart, who is in her thirty-first season as a Festival stage manager, "one when you are in the rehearsal hall and the other when you get on stage."

The first day on stage, she says, tends to be gentle and exploratory. "What you want to discover now are

Left: Brian Scott, stage manager of *Jesus Christ Superstar*. Right: Melissa Rood, assistant stage manager of *Jesus Christ Superstar*. Facing page: Jaz Sealey (Curio) and production stage manager Margaret Palmer backstage during a performance of *Twelfth Night*.

the problems. How is the stage different from the rehearsal hall? What did you do in the rehearsal hall that seemed so great that doesn't work at all on stage?"

The stage manager also works with the director, the designer, the lighting designer and the sound designer as they set levels and cues for lighting and sound. Actors aren't present for this; instead, people with the exotic-sounding job of "light walkers" stand in for them (silently) on stage so that the lights can be properly focused.

"We go in front of the public with a very polished show"

"Then comes the great day when you put it all together: the cue-to-cue," says Stuart. At this point they run only the sections of the play that involve cues: lighting changes, sound effects, actors' entrances and exits. The next step is the tech run, when they do the whole play with all the technical aspects—ideally, without stopping. Then the tech dress, when they add costumes and try the quick changes, which may need work. Either the costume needs to be adjusted so that it's easier to get out of, or more people are needed to help make the change. Sometimes it's as simple as just setting things out in a different place. After that is the first dress rehearsal, which is usually closed.

By that time, says Stuart, "you want to be in running mode. Because the actors need that. You want to have your problems solved." The second dress rehearsal often has an invited audience: friends, colleagues, family. And then comes the first public preview.

"We go in front of the public with a very polished show," says Stuart. "You may have improvements in mind: you want to see the public's reaction and fine tune some details. While we certainly don't regard it as a *finished* product, it's meant to be a *polished* product."

Above: Buddy T. Dog in rehearsal for *The Best Brothers* (2012). Facing page: Trainer Dan Frankian of Hawkeye Bird and Animal Control with Clara the hawk from *Camelot*.

Finally, opening night arrives. Thirty-five minutes before curtain, the stage manager checks that all the actors are there, then she goes up into her booth to call the show.

The popular impression of a stage manager is usually of someone standing in the wings who delivers a prompt when an actor "dries"—forgets the next line. While prompting is part of the job, it very rarely happens.

"I've only prompted once in my life," says Stuart. "The actor was talking—it was during a long speech, then all of a sudden he said, 'Line.' There was that moment. I thought, 'This isn't happening. I've been here for twenty-five seasons. They can't be calling me for a line now.' So I gave him the line, and he said maybe half a line, and then again he said, 'Line.' So I gave him the line again and he managed to keep going that time.

Productions involving animals present their own unique challenges

"I felt so guilty. I thought maybe I'd given him the wrong line. But I was taping the show because it was a preview. And I watched the tape, and I realized that although I'd given him the right line and it was at an adequate volume, it wasn't adequate to penetrate the state he was in; he was so wrapped up in his role."

Productions involving animals—such as Clara, the hawk in *Camelot*—present their own unique challenges. Cindy Toushan, who was stage manager for *Camelot*, recalls that Clara "pooped every day before the show. She almost pooped on cue. The handlers bring her out, we talk to her and she poops. It was part of the routine. She was a very vocal bird, so she squawked a lot backstage."

Toushan has vivid memories of working with animals at other theatres too. "I did an opera with a hawk," she

says, "so I've done two show hawks. I've done two white stallions pulling a carriage, a pig, a lamb, a lot of dogs. I did an opera once that had a vulture, a monkey, three puppies and two children. The monkey would poop down the back of the tenor's jacket every day. We had to block the show so that the tenor never turned around."

Shows with children in the cast can be challenging too, if not quite so messy. "I did *The King and I* here with nineteen children. *Oliver!* had sixteen. I did *Hansel and Gretel* in Toronto with forty-eight kids. That's a lot of kids. They add a whole other layer."

"The better the stage management team is, the less you know they are there"

What makes a great stage manager isn't easy to pin down. Certainly a sense of organization and an innate calmness are necessary. "You need to be able to take the temperature of the room," says Nora Polley, who was a stage manager at Stratford for thirty-seven seasons and now works in the Archives. There are a lot of egos, some of them delicate. "One of the biggest things is consistency. Stage management needs to be consistent and reliable."

There is an element of nurturing, too. "You have to be the type of person who likes to take care of people," says Toushan, "because you touch every person involved in the production, and they all have their own agendas, they all have their own needs, they all have their own approaches, and you have to be able to cope with that. There is a range of what you're responsible for. First, you're responsible for health and safety, secondly the artistic integrity of the show, and the third thing is morale. By the end of the season the performers

Facing page: Production stage manager Margaret Palmer and Sara Topham (Célimène) backstage during a performance of *The Misanthrope* (2011). Above: Chilina Kennedy (Mary Magdalene) and stage manager Brian Scott during a rehearsal for *Jesus Christ Superstar*.

The. John Grey in the stage management office at the Festival Theatre.

have had everything: broken wrists, cancer, flu, deaths in the family, births. And in the middle of all that mess you have to keep the show going."

Some ability as a mind-reader is also a definite asset. "The more we can anticipate what they need for the next day," says Toushan, "the smoother it goes. I firmly believe the better the stage management team is, the less you know they are there. Everything just happens—like the theatre fairies came in and it magically happened. They don't even have to ask; it is sitting right there."

Theatre is a social act, and most social acts contain an element of risk. You can be embraced or rejected, hugged or lynched. There are awkward moments, polite applause and the tsunami surge of a spontaneous ovation. There can be sickness, injury, infighting and miscues. In theatre, like life, your mistakes can occasionally be hidden (dropped lines, missed lighting cues), other times not (falling off the stage). Most mistakes can be forgiven, but not all of them can be erased. But through it all, the stage manager's job is to keep an imagined world on stage unfolding as effortlessly and as seamlessly as possible—and to do so invisibly.

"The general public doesn't know we exist," Ann Stuart says, "and we don't *want* them to know that we exist. We want to take them away from their lives."

She adds: "I think of myself as part of a loop that channels all the different elements and holds them together. Like that piece of grey cable that leads into your telephone: if you open that up, there's a red strand and a green strand and a black strand and a yellow strand. But the grey tube holds them all together. The stage manager holds all the elements together: the lighting, the sound, the special effects, the traps, the pyrotechnics. And the actors, in the sense that you largely control their entrances and their exits.

"And when you're calling a show, it's like a current that flows through you. It flows through you to the stage, and then it comes back to you. It's like you're a part of some kind of circle."

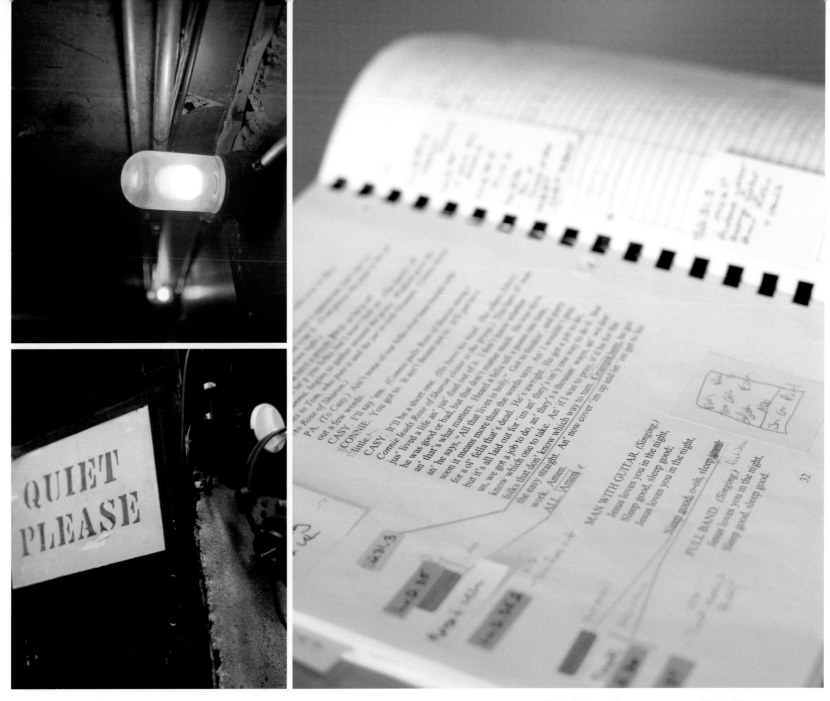

Top left: A backstage cue light—when it goes on, the actor prepares to make an entrance; when it goes off, that's his or her cue to enter. Right: The stage manager's "bible," or prompt book, for *The Grapes of Wrath* (2011).

Vocal and movement coaches and dozens of others work behind the scenes in the service of the directors. And the directors work in service of the text. They are all in the service, ultimately, of the theatre

Epilogue

One of the recurring themes among Festival employees is the concept of invisibility: we are doing a good job if you don't notice us. Gerry Altenburg, Head of Wigs and Makeup, says: "Some of our toughest and best work is the stuff that goes unnoticed. *The Little Years*, for example—for the most part, you don't really notice they're wearing wigs." Sound designers strive to go unnoticed, preferring to enhance the production rather than draw attention to the sound. Stage managers concur. "The general public doesn't know we exist," says Ann Stuart, "and we don't *want* them to know we exist." If they are noticed, it's because something went wrong. Lighting designer Michael Walton echoes this thought. "Most people don't notice lighting design unless it's bad," he says. The invisibility extends, surprisingly, to the actors. "At its best," Sara Topham says, "acting is invisible." Vocal and movement coaches and dozens of others work behind the scenes in the service of the directors. And the directors work in service of the text.

The underlying idea is that the audience shouldn't see the strings. The theatre is a curious combination of the real (it happens live, in real time) and a suspension of disbelief (that we are in sixteenth-century Illyria watching a man in lurid 1920s golf clothes drunkenly trying to sink a putt, as we were in *Twelfth Night*). Most of the hundreds of people whose names are listed in small print in every house program not only work in anonymity but strive for it. They are all in the service, ultimately, of the theatre, of that singular experience.

This book has offered snapshots of some of those people. There are many others, including those who work long hours in administration and fundraising and marketing. At the height of the season, Stratford employs over a thousand people. The Stratford Shakespeare Festival has grown considerably since the tent overlooking the Avon River was erected in 1953, and literally tens of thousands of people have contributed to its success.

Facing page: Company member Victor Dolhai prepares to make an entrance in *The Misanthrope* (2011). Above: Juan Chioran (Philinte) and Ben Carlson (Aceste) pass the time between their scenes in *The Misanthrope*.

Facing page: A *Jesus Christ Superstar* rehearsal seen from the wings stage right. Above: Hard day's knights? Julius Sermonia (foreground) and other members of the Round Table take a break backstage during a performance of *Camelot*.

Above left: Steve Ross (Clitandre) backstage during a performance of *The Misanthrope* (2011). Above right: Jonathan Winsby (Lancelot) stays connected backstage during a performance of *Camelot*. Facing page: Lighting designer Michael Walton works on *42nd Street* (2012) at the Festival Theatre.

If success is measured by audience size, then Stratford is a resounding hit, attracting tens of millions of people in its sixty-year history. Certainly, the excellence of the artists Stratford attracts to work on its stages is another measure of that success, and the keystone of it.

The Stratford Shakespeare Festival has grown considerably since the tent overlooking the Avon River was erected in 1953, and literally tens of thousands of people have contributed to its success

Stratford's founding Artistic Director, Tyrone Guthrie, articulated the vision that first attracted those artists when he called theatre "the oldest social, moral and political platform in the world." No theatre has longevity without a strong reason for existing, and Guthrie passed that torch to his protégé and successor, Michael Langham, who in turn passed it along to his successors. Stratford's present Artistic Director, Des McAnuff, counts Langham as one of his most important mentors, and McAnuff's successor, Antoni Cimolino, who will become Artistic Director in 2013, was mentored by McAnuff's predecessor, Richard Monette.

"What's past is prologue." The Festival's 2012 Visitors' Guide announces the sixtieth season with those words. It is a season that includes a two-thousand-year-old Greek play that helped ignite Roman drama, which in turn served as the model for Shakespeare and his contemporaries. The great playwright Thornton Wilder called theatre "a torch race" and readily admitted to borrowing from those who came before him, including Molière in this season's *The Matchmaker*. There are three plays by Shakespeare in the 2012 season, and Shakespeare's forms and preoccupations in turn can be seen in the contemporary work that appears on Stratford stages this season.

Henry V is the culmination of Shakespeare's great eight-play study of leadership in English history; *The War of 1812* is part of Michael Hollingsworth's twenty-one-part play cycle that defines Canadian identity by re-examining its history. *Cymbeline* is part of a series of plays in which Shakespeare examines fathers and daughters; Daniel MacIvor's *The Best Brothers* takes a look at mothers and sons. Gilbert and Sullivan set the mark for an unbridled exuberance in *The Pirates of Penzance* that can be seen in three other musicals Stratford is presenting this season. Christopher Plummer's one-man show *A Word or Two* is a homage to the writers who inspired and helped mould this great artist; Alon Nashman and Paul Thompson's *Hirsch* is a homage to the extraordinary passions and legacy of one of Stratford's Artistic Directors.

What's past is prologue. "By staging classics and new plays side by side," McAnuff believes, "you are reminded that classics are not museum pieces. They also spoke to issues contemporary to the times in which they were written, and playwrights who are writing today are exploring issues that our predecessors wrote about centuries ago." And so the torch race continues as the marathon story of the Stratford Shakespeare unfolds into the future, nurtured by the beehive of activity that we celebrate in this book.

Acknowledgements

I would like to thank all those at the Stratford Shakespeare Festival who gave so generously of their time and expertise. Neil Cheney's patience in the scene shop was deeply appreciated, as were the tutorials from Cynthia Toushan and The. John Gray. A special thanks goes to Dr. Francesca Marini, who conducted many of the interviews for this book, and whose tours and knowledge were instrumental in understanding the scope of the Festival. Robert Blacker deserves praise for his deft editing of the manuscript. I would especially like to thank David Prosser, whose ongoing editorial guidance and deep understanding of the Festival, and of the theatre, were invaluable in the writing of this book.

– *Don Gillmor*

For the Stratford Shakespeare Festival . . .

In addition to those named above, General Director Antoni Cimolino and Artistic Director Des McAnuff wish to express their warmest thanks to Don Gillmor and Erin Samuell; to Krista Dodson and Andy Foster for their creative roles in the design of this book; to Dean Gabourie, Jason Miller, Judith Richardson and the Archives staff; and to Anita Gaffney and Michael Levine for the parts they played in bringing the project together.

Their thanks go also to all the Festival artists, artisans, staff and crew who directly participated in the making of this book, and to all the others on whose extraordinary talent, skill and dedication every season depends.

And finally, they extend their very special thanks to you: the patrons, Members and donors without whose generous and loyal support the extraordinary artistic enterprise celebrated in these pages simply could not exist.

Additional Photography

Page 6: Terry Manzo. Page 9: Jane Edmonds. Pages 47 and 56: Scott Wishart, *The Beacon Herald*. Page 59: David Hou. Page 62: CBC, *The Hour*. Page 64: Terry Manzo. Page 65: Scott Wishart, *The Beacon Herald*. Page 82 (bottom right): David Hou. Page 88: Krista Dodson. Page 94: Richard Bain. Pages 100 and 101: Terry Manzo. Page 107 (top right): Krista Dodson. Page 110: David Hou. Pages 112, 118, 119 (bottom left and right) and 122: Krista Dodson. Page 124 (top left and right): Terry Manzo. Pages 123 (bottom right), 135 and 148 (bottom left): Krista Dodson. Page 153: Terry Manzo. Pages 155 (bottom right) and 156 (bottom): Krista Dodson. Page 168: Burdett Photography. Page 172 (top right): Kerry Hayes. Page 179: David Hou.

A view from backstage during a performance of *The Grapes of Wrath*.